This book is dedicated with love to Kumud Mody
wife, partner, adviser and friend

HOW TO MAKE MILLIONS
WITHOUT A CENT
IN YOUR POCKET

HOW TO MAKE MILLIONS WITHOUT A CENT IN YOUR POCKET

(A PRACTICAL GUIDE TO SUCCESS IN REAL ESTATE)

Dr. ANIL MODY

First published in 1995

Typeset by Macmillan India Ltd., Madras-2
Printed by Thomson Press (India) Ltd., Faridabad

Table of contents

(The forms contained in summation (Appendix A to D) may be somewhat different in different countries. However, the basic character of these remain same.)

Profile – Anil Mody

Anil Mody came to Canada from India in October 1960 after completing B.A., L.L.B., and M.Com. from the University of Bombay with only $ 7.00 in his pocket. He studied at the McGill University and Sir George Williams University in Montreal, where he did his B.Com., C.M.A. (a professional accountant degree). While in Montreal, he worked with an American Company, the United Shoe Machinery Corporation (U.S.M.C.), for 12 years and came to Ottawa in October 1972 to join the federal government. He also studied the real estate market and started investing in the same. Slowly and steadily he expanded his investments, thereby acquiring many properties, including a shopping plaza.

Even at the time of recession, when many people have been affected badly, Mody has acquired more properties and expanded his investment in real estate. He says that he was lucky to have the support of his wife, Kumud, from the start as well as two brothers (Chandrakant and Vipul) and son (Parimal), who are now looking after the daily operations.

He has always been there for any friends or relatives who were interested in real estate.

Anil Mody, entrepreneur par excellence, *a self-made million-aire*, has been a senior federal civil servant in Ottawa for over 22 years.

He came to Canada in 1960 for further studies at the McGill University. His romance and tribulations in those distant years, as an impoverished immigrant and a student, are solid testament to the success—both personal and finanical—that he has achieved.

As an accountant, a lawyer, a civil servant, a real estate investor, Mody set out milestones of achievement that do credit to all who wish to follow his example.

Mody, the achiever, has relentlessly followed one principle in all his endeavours: Be humane and kind to others. His rewards attest to the wisdom of this dictum.

His book, "How to make millions without a cent in your pocket", is not just a ordinary real estate book, nor is it a "get rich quick", prescription, it is a chronology of a single individual's effort to shape his future by addressing the god-given will, strength and capacity.

Mody's efforts to tell his readers that what he has achieved is not a miracle but that, given the proper know-how and the will, anyone can replicate the same success, if not more.

Mody, married, with two children, and lives in Ottawa, Canada.

CHAPTER 1

In the beginning

Early on, as a boy from modest but comfortable middle class family in Western India, I was acutely aware that, to get on in this world, to make a millionaire out of myself, I would have to work hard and work smart.

The school days were challenging and I did very well indeed. From school to university in India, hard work and determination paid off handsomely. I took my Masters in Commerce and then graduated from Law School. That was no mean achievement in India, where thousands upon thousands come to the universities, because that perhaps is the only way to a secure job and, hopefully, a decent lifestyle.

In my case, with graduation, the windows of opportunity seemed to open as if by magic. I could pick and choose a job. But the enticement of studies abroad came my way. A degree from the western world was a sure guarantee to a secure, upwardly mobile career in India. For me, it also represented an opportunity that was tailor-made for my future plans to the road to affluence and even prosperity.

The odyssey began with a short stopover in London, England. But, fate and circumstances conspired, and ultimately, I headed for Canada, Montreal to be precise. I planned to enroll with the famous McGill University and study commerce, accounting and, eventually, law.

It was early fall in Canada; but to my warm, tropical blood, the weather was pretty cold. I cannot recall any lasting first impression beyond that discomfort.

Be that as it may, this was Canada, the land of Kipling's desolation and the land of dreams and aspirations for all other migrants from the four corners of the world. Even so, Canada to me smelled like a land of opportunity, in fact, a land to be a millionaire, despite that impersonal airport atmosphere. I was stimulated. I could feel the fire of determination and impatience in my heart. There was a new kind of hunger in my heart for greater and better things to happen. And there was also hunger in my stomach. It had been hours since the last meal.

The reality of this hunger soon enough pushed everything else into the background for later, sober perspective. This reality was pregnant with some urgency and many problems.

As a newcomer in town, I did not know a single soul, and nobody seemed to notice or care. A quick check into my pockets revealed that I had about seven dollars in assorted changes with which to take care, as best as I could, of my immediate needs. But these needs called for, among others, transportation to the city, some warm clothing, a reasonable accommodation, and food.

The basic needs represented the very first financial decisions I would have to make in Canada. Well, it was scary, but it was challenging. At least, that is how I tried to look at these problems in the first few hours of my life in Canada.

I decided that a healthy hike to the city would take care of the cold, might even dull the hunger for food, besides taking me to my destination.

The only problem remaining, that is, housing, was taken care of after a surprisingly quick search. I was installed in a windowless closet-sized accommodation in a rooming house for a princely sum of eighteen dollars a month.

Humble as the shelter was, it was comfortable because I had planned only to sleep there at nights. On a large measure, at least temporarily, the matter of cold Canadian weather was also taken care of. As for food, as a confirmed vegetarian,

I could see no major problem. I was all set to make the appointment with my destiny.

Although my parents in India were by no means wealthy, they had decided to make the supreme investment on my future by undertaking the difficult task of financing a better part of my tuition fees. This still called for the fullest application of my facilities and skills of survival and to become a wage earner at a short notice in a very new land.

The very next day, having visited the university to take care of registration, course selection and other formalities, I began an intensive job search. Success came surprisingly easily. As an accountant, I was able to secure a part time job. The pay, for me, a newcomer, was very good indeed. It paid my rent, fed me adequately, and also left some loose change for saving.

A pattern of dual life was established that I would follow to this day. I studied hard for my Bachelor degree in Commerce at Sir George Williams (now Concordia University), and, eventually, did extremely well. Later, I studied for my R.I.A. (now C.M.A.) to become a professional accountant at McGill University in Montreal. All through these times, I also held, at times, more than one job, generally in the afternoons, evenings and weekends.

I was not affluent, not by a long shot. But I was no longer a penniless stranger to this new land, Canada. I could see that dreams of becoming a real life millionaire could be made to come true.

With reasonable financial stability and security, I found the hard grind of daily routine somewhat oppressive at times. Although I had become quite proficient in juggling various jobs and studies through efficient time management, the saps on energy occasionally took a nosedive.

I began to miss someone dear to me, who had entered my life not so long ago. Before leaving India, I was married to a petite, pretty lab technician. Increasingly, I was missing her, especially on those bone-tired lonely nights in that windowless closet, masquerading as a room.

Now that I was making a reasonable living through various part-time jobs and doing well in my studies, I felt confident of facing the future challenges much better and far strongly if my bride were to be at my side, sharing the joys of victories and the agonies of defeats as we together mapped the blueprint of our life.

In October 1961, my bride joined me. The pleasure of having her with me was but short-lived. The conjugal bliss was too soon invaded by economies of reality. My supposed affluence allowed us to move out of the closet to a small apartment. The pressure of finances also increased as we began to set up a reasonable family life. I began working at three jobs and walked several miles each day, fair or foul weather, to and from and between jobs and our home. Even so, it was not enough to provide a reasonable degree of comfort to my wife, who incidentally, was a child of a wealthy family back home. I was extremely fortunate in pairing with a partner in life who was as spirited and ambitious as I. She would be a source of encouragement, strength, counsellor and friend all my life.

The second phase of our life together in Canada began with a challenge. This time, I was not alone, my wife was right there. She had been trained as a lab technician in India. Now she too began to look for a job. Within a short time, she was employed as a lab technician. Our combined income took some pressure off the affairs of home-making. Our apartment, consisting of one room, cost us thirty dollars a month, but that place was ours, and held many fond memories over all these years.

By 1966, I had completed my studies and had acquired degrees in business and commerce. My status as a student in Canada was easily changed into landed immigrant. This now enabled me to seek and accept full-time employment. The financial situation suddenly became very rosy indeed.

And a good thing too! The year 1967 was the year of Expo and Montreal was the tourist attraction of the year. Among many notable visitors, there was General de Gaulle. We also had my parents to visit us. In keeping with the north American tradition and to prove to my parents that I was climbing to the top of the world, I bought my very first car, a battered old Volkswagen, for a couple of hundred dollars. It worked fine and my parents were suitably impressed.

It was a good visit. My parents were very pleased with our modest success. Soon, however, they left. Unlike de Gaulle, they did not cause any political confusion.

The politeness of my parents, of course, was overshadowed by the rudeness of the General and its violent aftereffect in Montreal, the city that was embodiment of Canada to me, a scared visitor back in 1967.

The Separatist faction in the province of Quebec took on a violent character. The English-speaking residents were fearful of a possible uncertain future. Business concerns and individuals alike were planning to leave, or actually leaving, the "la Belle provence."

My wife and I were not too sure what the best move would be. As luck would have it, a former acquaintance and colleague, who had earlier moved to Ottawa to work with the federal government, on a chance encounter, suggested that a move out of Quebec into Ontario, preferably to Ottawa, would be wise.

Since we were off and on thinking in terms of Toronto as our next move, I decided to look into the federal government employment situation in Ottawa. Surprisingly, it took less effort than expected.

Just four years into its existence, the federal Department of Regional Economic Expansion was just getting ready for major reorganization and reorientation. This department dealt with the regions on development matters and was responsible for managing billions of dollars annually. My academic background in management, accounting and law, along with a thorough understanding of the principles of cost efficiency or effectiveness, were readily accepted by the federal government. So, in 1972, I came to Ottawa as a bureaucrat. This would be the city where I would make my future home and build my fortune.

There was a slight problem, however. My wife, loving and loved as she was, refused to leave Montreal and move with me to Ottawa. She was adamant and insisted that we bought a house and set up a proper home for our two children.

Like every man, I was all in favour of owning a home. The problem was that I did not have the necessary money to pay for one. Faced with my dear wife's odd behaviour, I began to take stock of my material wealth. By cashing in all my modest investments in bonds and by selling off every bit of things we owned, I came up with little over $10,000.

The next hurdle was to find a proper house that was affordable and acceptable. Near Walkley and Russel Road, a new housing complex was developing. There was only one house up and the price was right. For a price of $35,000 and $10,000 down payment, I could take possession of it rightway. So far so good. The only drawback was that the innards of the house, like utilities, were not in place. The water had to be carted in from some place, the electricity flowed from nearby sales office of the developer. Also, there was no other house occupied other than ours.

No matter. My wife was happy and we moved into our first, brand new home. We were to be there for a very long time, raising a family.

Immediately after the move, however, we found our evenings somewhat of a drag. Just by ourselves, we were like a marooned couple.

Soon enough, after evening meals, I got into the habit of dropping in by the sales office to say hello to the people—the only people around. He would talk about house building, about real estate market in Ottawa and I would listen to the conversations of the sales staff with prospective buyers. Before long, I began to learn the business, from bare nails up. I also got a good understanding of the psychological aspects of sales techniques. Above all, right in front of my own eyes, I could see an economic miracle take shape.

The volatility of real estate prices is one of the characteristics of this business. But, until then, I had no perception of the sharp swings that were an integral part of this game. Within three months, the price of my own house had increased by over $5,000.

It intrigued me and challenged my good old ambition for an affluent financial independence by becoming a millionaire. I decided to study the real estate market in general and the market in Ottawa in particular. Could it be the vehicle to fulfil my dream?

The exploration for an answer began, logically enough, with a community college course on real estate. At the same time, I began to spend a lot of time at the public library, reading the available books and articles on Canadian and American real estate. The local newspapers were also a part of daily reading menu. On weekends, visits to open houses and to residential construction sites, to talk to the construction and sales people, was a must. I felt that the community college course on theories of real estate market ought to be supplemented by as much practical, real-world information. In this assessment I was not wrong. I came out of the course with flying colors and a very real idea as to how, at last, the seed of my financial success could be sowed.

The ground had been well prepared, I felt. I put a time frame of 15 years. I hoped that within this time frame I would realize my lifelong dream and become a millionaire.

As an exploratory first step, I joined in equal partnership with a friend and began to look for a suitable house to buy. Such a house was found, bought and sold within a few weeks.

We came out of the deal with a clear profit of $3,000 for each partner. It was a successful test case and a great boost to my confidence. I was ready for solo runs.

In the spring of 1973, armed with a line of credit based on the appreciated market value of my home, which was by now worth $45,000—a net $10,000 increase—and a loan of $7,500 from the C.S. Coop against my federal government salary, I was ready to meet the Ottawa real estate market. The hunt ended at a condo complex that was being completed in the city's west end at the waterfront. For starter, I bought one condo unit for $24,000, with $1,000 deposit. The salesperson I was dealing with was very persuasive, fortunately. On his insistence, I ended up buying two more units in that complex. In retrospect, that was a good decision and also the beginning of a completely new and satisfying venture. I felt the intoxicating bite of sales and purchases and the rewarding profits.

Early on, I was doubtful of the third party—the middleman—in a transaction. It only boosted the price and ate away the resulting profits. Consequently, I began an intensive search of the local newspapers and their real estate sections, along with scouting of the city section by section, division by division.

Somewhat accidentally, I stumbled on a very curious fact that, in Hull, on the Quebec side of the Ottawa river, for some peculiar reason, the property values were nearly $12–14 thousand less. Clearly, the situation called for a more critical examination.

I got down to this examination with the earnestness of a gold prospector of a bygone era. I studied the housing markets in Hull, Gatineau and Aylmer, talked to the local residents, municipal politicians, business people and the developers. It transpired that, for some psychological reasons, over the past several decades, the value and the prices of equivalent properties in Ottawa and the "wrong" side of the Ottawa river remained different: the "wrong" side having a lower—by some $14,000—property value. On the other hand, the rental aspects, that is, demand and rental worth, on both sides of the river were similar.

At long last, the Canadian promise and opportunity were handed to me on a proverbial silver platter. I was now convinced that the "wrong" side of the Ottawa River held the right key to my financial success.

As a first step to exploit the situation, I contacted my associates and friends to join with me in equal partnership. While most agreed with my assessment, only two finally decided to take the plunge.

The second step was most crucial. The first buy had to be the harbinger of the success to come. Following intensive search, eventually, in 1973, I bought the first house in Aylmer, for $13,000. In Ottawa area, the same property was going for a minimum of $24,000. I had no difficulty in renting it out almost immediately. And at a handsome rent too!

I decided not to touch another property in the Ottawa area. Instead, my efforts and investments would concentrate in Hull-Gatineau-Aylmer area. The opportunities for bigger and better rates of return were hard to overlook.

Even as my property holdings were increasing, I did not for one moment think of quitting my job and the source of steady, handsome salary with the federal government. In order not to jeopardize my efficiency at work, I had to work on my real estate dealings in the evenings and on weekends. This was no hardship. I had done worse during my student days in Montreal.

Frequent contacts with the city's financial institutions not only eased the problems of access to quick finances, I was also offered a very lucrative job as the Head of the real estate section of a leading Trust Company. I preferred to be my own master.

Subsequent to my decision to concentrate in Hull–Gatineau–Aylmer area and having made few property purchases, I was faced with yet another strategic dilemma. Up to now, I was content in acquiring the property. As a result, I was travelling considerable distances in different directions. Time was being wasted. I had to focus on a deliberately selected target area and concentrate there all future acquisitions.

The decision of a target area for acquisition was based on some very natural considerations. The area had to be within easy commuting distance from Ottawa-Hull, the hub of the area's business and federal government activities; the area also had to be of interest to, and focus of, new and growing construction activities, and, of course, the area had to have an established community to begin with.

Having made the decision as well as considered the overriding conditions, I began an extensive search in the Hull-Gatineau-Aylmer area. Finally, I settled on "Project Le Barron" in Gatineau and an area 3 to 4 square miles in radius from the Project. This was an ideal site. It had a well-established community of mostly middle-income employees of either the federal government or the business sector. New construction activities were booming because, in part, the federal government's massive move away from traditional Ottawa center to the "wrong" side of the river in Hull.

By then, I had four or five properties in this area. During the next few months, the list of acquisitions grew. Contrary to fears expressed by others, I had not experienced any difficulty in renting out these properties.

As my real estate investment grew, I felt a different kind of pressure. Since my acquaintances and friends tended to back away from the business association I offered, I was working out alone. At times, the burden of decision seemed to become too heavy.

Ever perceptive and helpful, my wife solved this growing problem of possible burn-out. She was prepared to give up her former training as a lab technician and opt for training in real estate investment. She took the course and completed with some distinction. Now, I could discuss problems with her: seek her advise and even, if needed, let her handle some business matters. As a husband and wife team, our venture flourished.

As we became more experienced in the business, we decided not to participate in the summer buying season, when everyone was a potential buyer and, thus, the market was kept artificially high. Instead, we concentrated on winter buying, when the potential seller was likely to negotiate a selling price more to our advantage.

During the summer lull, we made it a practice to look for capital, to meet with local politicians, lawyers, notaries and business people. This was a conscious and planned move to widen our circle of potential support and help, contributing directly or indirectly to our growing investment.

During winter months, we were not just out to buy the available properties. We made it a point to be very cautious and judicious about our prospects. However, we used to visit—and still do—as many "Houses For Sale", just to know about, and get the feel, of the properties and their characters.

As a general rule, for the properties that we liked, we made offers of low down payments, especially for those that were left vacant and unoccupied. On many occasions, to our surprise, we were the only bidders and, thus, were able to "pick up" a few properties at very low prices indeed.

At about this time, when we had amassed a large number of properties, we tried out another gambit. In instances where we were the only prospective buyers, we signed the purchase and sale agreements accompanying a low dollar down payment and with the explicit provision to close the deal in 3 to 6 months hence. This enabled us to scout for and find necessary finances as well as to locate a tenant without incurring any direct costs to us.

Whether these methods of real estate operation are textbook-prescribed or not, they have worked superbly well for us during the past two or more decades. I would be the first one to declaim any connotation to business genius as I would readily downplay any suggestion of divine guidance. All I know is that it has been a long period of hard work and an astute application of the knowledge so doggedly acquired.

As we stand on the brink of the next decade and the new century, I am pleased and proud that Canada has granted us the opportunity promised to make a fortune.

Yes, I stand a financially successful and secure person. On the way to this point, I have had to be hard, practical, but never ruthless, to my fellow human beings.

That in itself is a lesson and a subject for another book. You don't have to be a cut-throat to achieve financial success. You can remain a human being.

In this book, however, I wish to share with my readers the simple rules of game that have worked so well for me. I do believe that one does not have to be a financial wizard or genius to secure a reasonably successful financial nest-egg.

I invite you, the reader, to study the following pages and discover for yourself that the "magic" of being a millionaire is within your means and, more importantly, within your reach.

CHAPTER 2

Objective: success

A decision, be that on your career or on financial security, is a critical element. In fact, a decision is the cornerstone on which to build. The quality of this decision will ultimately determine the quality of the final outcome.

A decision is made, not lightly, nor on impulse, but on careful preparation. This preparation involves gathering of information, familiarization of this evaluated information into knowledge, and, finally, determination, leading to search for opportunity.

We all know that none of these happen overnight: one must have patience. Once the seed has been planted in the fertile ground and has the guarantee of proper care, there is no way on the Earth to stop the seed from germinating, the seedling from growing, the plant from flowering, and, ultimately, from bearing fruit.

The same process holds for all human endeavors. True, the very lucky ones do short circuit the process and reach certain goals, but these goals generally have proven to be rather short-lived. Records show that instant millionaires from lottery wins, like chinese fire crackers, tend to come down to earth often worse-off than before.

The decision-making process is a fearsomely pompous word, its meaning is very simple however. It means that a decision has to be made, based on a proper use of specific information, objectives and goals to be reached, and a step-by-step plan or strategy to reach these goals and objectives. The necessary back-up resources have to be looked into— things like what is needed, how much is readily available, where to get them in quick and ready supply. Again, it is just like planting the seed. You want to know what kind of plant you wish to have, where to plant it, whether the soil is good, the availability of light, air, water, and the availability of proper care and protection. Given an assurance of all these, the seed will grow. Given an assurance of, and access to, necessary resources, any decision to reach any objective or goal will succeed. There is no other condition.

A decision to succeed must also be backed up with one hundred percent solid and pure determination. Come hell or high water, this determination must not waver. Such determination is called by many names, among them, faith. Do you remember what Jesus said about absolute determination or faith? "If you have faith the size of a grain of mustard, you can move the mountain". It is worth remembering.

I am not a philosopher, nor am I a religious fanatic: however, I am a practitioner of faith—in whatever I am doing at any given time. Again and again, a carefully planned decision, backed with determination and necessary commitment of resources, has been outstandingly successful in all my business and personal ventures.

At the time, I was not aware of all the elements that have gone into ensuring those successes. Later examinations, each time, proved the validity of each of the assertions that I have made in these pages. It only goes to show that (a) it is in our nature to be instinctively calculating, cautious and venturesome; (b) all our actions are, by and large, carefully organized and goal-oriented, and (c) given the achievable practicality and the necessary ingredients, any undertaking can be successful, for any one.

As in everything having something to do with our lives, the desire to succeed, universal as it is for every single man or woman, the determination, of which I spoke earlier, is subject to far too many intimidating external circumstances; look, for instance, at the gigantic success of Donald Trump. Intimidation comes from the fact that we always look at the end result and conveniently forget or refuse to look beyond the end result, at the very origin, that, combined with determination, planning, hard work, failures, among others, has charted the course for a dazzling success. Donald Trump himself, in his books, has glorified the early beginnings with all the failures and heartbreaks, rather than the end result. This end result is the fruit of labor—for most notable successes. You may look into the lives of now-successful and famous, artists, movie stars, authors, business magnates, among others, and you will be amazed by the pressure of hardship and poverty they all had to surmount rather than abandon such aspirations as impractical or unachievable.

Surely, such dedication and single-minded determination are God's gift. Without such gift, our cultures and our civilization would be so much more drab and colorless: our economic and social lifestyles would not have progressed, perhaps, beyond pre-stone age; our human achievements that allow us the claim to being "made in the image of God" would have been no less than presumptuous.

Human ingenuity, coupled with dedication and determination, has been at the very root of the evolution of human kind and the growth of our successive civilizations. This quality is within every single one of us. It lies dormant, to be awakened by the weight and intensity of an individual's will to fulfil a dream or a purpose.

Unfortunately for humanity, not all but only a few have been able to prolong and sustain the demands imposed on us. Most of us, gifted as we all are, capitulate too soon in the face of the nature of sacrifice that is invariably demanded of us before "success" is within our grasp.

As a result, we are tempted, and tend, to attribute the mystic quality of success to those few who are successful. There is, of course, nothing wrong in capitulation after an honest struggle to achieve our goal. Ideally, those of us who fail in our efforts should take pride in the very fact we have struggled; instead, we tend to suffer from a lifelong sense of frustration and insignificance, especially while comparing ourselves with those successful. This attitude has an overall negative social and psychological effect on many. We become discontent and, in consequence, we become even less success-oriented in the matter of day-to-day living and in interactions with others, be they within the family, in the work place or with the society at large.

In my own personal life, I have attempted to undertake and achieve some degree of success in many areas. In these undertakings, I have always given the very best of my efforts. But that has not been enough, not every time, either because of lack of sufficient information or knowledge, lack of ingredients necessary to build the steep steps to success, or simply because my own heart and soul were not totally and completely committed to such undertakings.

What I am trying to emphasize is that while it is impossible to turn a crow into a peacock, it is certainly within the realm of probability to teach the crow to behave like a crow and do successfully what the crows may be adept at doing. It is important to recognize and realize our own limitations as well as our special attributes and abilities. Once they have been recognized, developed and sharpened, it is likely to be difficult to be a failure. A flower, given the required nurturing, cannot but bloom.

It is also important to make a special note before concluding this chapter, that there are areas where anyone with a certain degree of determination, information and preparation can achieve a life or a lifestyle that can be called comfortable and reasonably successful in the sense that economic worries can be minimized or even eliminated. Such an achievement or success may not be comparable to that enjoyed by the likes of Donald

Trump, but what is wrong in not becoming a Trump? The ultimate success in our lives does not rest upon how large the bank balance is, but rather, on how comfortably one can enjoy life and all the attributes of an enjoyable, peaceful and productive life. It is o.k. to fix one's eyes on the shining distant stars, but most of us must, sooner rather than later, lower our gaze and explore the alternative to achieve the means of creating a comfortable, enjoyable life.

What follows hereon is not a philosophical discourse on the invisible and intangible qualities that make superstars of success of so few of our fellow human beings.

I have always taken to heart the immortal word of wisdom of Albert Einstein, a genius is 99% hard work and only 1% luck. I am sure, Einstein did not intend this profound observation only as a modest disclaimer for his genius qualities, but as a folksy guidance of reasonable success for all of us.

At the very beginning, I have related my own reasonable success, an assurance of comfortable and carefree life for my family and myself through cautious and calculated dealings in the real estate market in the national capital region of Canada. The dimension of my own success, compared to the modest beginning I made in Canada, is very substantial indeed, although by no means big enough to list me on the honour-roll of the Financial Post. It is not that I did not want it so, or that I have failed to achieve such a level of recognition, it is simply because such was never my objective. I looked for, and worked for, a level of social and economic security and independence that can be attained by any ordinary human being, including myself.

I do not seek the blazing glory of a Ford or a Rockefeller, nor crave for the greed of Hemesleys, but for a modest life of peace and financial security that, I personally believe, is the right of all, and can be achieved by any individual, provided he/she has a sense of dedication, commitment, willingness to work a little harder beyond the 9 to 5 routine, and, above all, has a definite and clear goal in view. This modest effort, a guide—if you like—is then for you to examine and find for yourself the destiny that awaits you.

CHAPTER 3

Any one can make a go of it

Although I am not a philosopher, it is my understanding that there is a philosopher in all of us, especially in those of us who come from far eastern origins, struggling to get out.

Having traced the humble beginning during that cold night in Montreal so many years ago, I believe I can be forgiven for playing the pseudo-philosopher in assessing the road I have followed to achieve my goal, the dream of a secure and comfortable life.

Canada, more than many other, is a land of opportunities. But these opportunities are not to be found like pennies on the sidewalk, nor are they lurking behind the bushes, waiting to be stumbled upon. No; we have to study our own lives very critically, to determine what exactly do we want and what it will do for us, and then, more importantly, we must ascertain what price are we prepared to pay. There is no fixed limit: it will be determined only by the nature of one's goals, on the intensity of one's desire to achieve them, and on the availability of internal and external resources for their attainment. I mean, you simply cannot go fishing, however badly you wish to catch one, without, at the very least, a fishing rod, complete with hook, line and sinkers as well as proper baits.

All worthwhile efforts in life are like that. That is why the word "quest"—grand as it is—fits so well for a just and well-prepared assault on the fortress of fortune and success.

I have learned from my own personal experience that the problem lies in the fact that we all want instant success, with little or no sacrifices, and, of course, with the best available fishing equipment. The costs and the logistics involved are enough to soften, even melt away, most hardened of determinations, in most instances, before the assault has begun.

Like the parable of Jesus, involving three servants, each given a copper coin by the master, we must have a sense of adventure, a jest for taking calculated risk, and some depth of understanding of what we are doing, where we are going and, above all, what exactly are we going to do when we get there.

The answers to these most basic questions in life are certainly different for each individual, but the ultimate answer or the ultimate goal, namely, what we are going to do when we reach wherever we set out to reach, is most assuredly the same, or similar in nature, for all of us: that we want success or the achievement of a dream and the pleasure of security and comfort that generally accompany all successes.

As an accountant/business administrator, I have been taught, not only in the Universities but also from experience in life, that, so long one can remain free of the destructive influence of obsession, of compulsive possessiveness, and single-minded ruthless pursuit of the highest peak of success, one can be successfully successful. There is no such thing as the highest peak of success, because the peak beyond the conquered one is always a bit more difficult, a bit more stiff. Such pursuit can cause only loneliness, unhappiness and leaves hardly any time or opportunity to enjoy the fruits of labor and success.

Success, of course, holds different meaning for different persons. My own modest origin and modest beginning have influenced positively what I would consider as success of my dreams and ambitions. In this dream, ambition, my family has played, and continues to play, a very central role. A lack of complete understanding of the family, especially of the spouse, is the prescription for catastrophe in one's personal life, when one ventures to keep appointment with destiny.

My wife has been a source of strength whenever I have felt weakened in my determination, she has always been there to comfort me when the harshness of the real world has overwhelmed me, she has given me peace of mind when I was troubled and she has patiently listened to me when I was confused. All of these are very necessary elements as we go after success. These qualities are priceless, you cannot buy or borrow them. They are carefully, lovingly home-grown.

It may sound trite or old-fashioned, but believe me, for the kind of success we all search and work, they are among the most important elements. A millionaire, with a cold, broken home is less successful than the day laborer with a loving, joyful home. What can you do with your millions, except perhaps become a jaded, dissatisfied, unfulfilled jet-setter surrounded with conniving friends who would as surely leave you, only to flock on to even richer victims of success?

Success, for most of us, is the fence that protects and even helps grow the joy of living in peace and in security among the loving and loyal circle of family and friends. Such a fence of success does not necessarily mean that one has to be a millionaire.

This is the central message that I want to share with you from the experience I have gained as I worked for my fence of success. I have been a working man—a professional—all my life. I have held a reasonably secure, challenging and interesting job with the Canadian Government. In the backdrop of a certain financial security from this job, I have carefully explored the various opportunities and prospects where a modest saving and the limited time, beyond 9 to 5, would allow me to search for the security of success I wished to provide for my growing family and for sun-set years.

In this exploration, my wife has been a willing and active partner. In order to augment our modest capital, she did not hesitate to take on part-time employments while the children were young. As they grew and were in school full time, my wife found full time employment.

The early days, as we began to collect the necessary material for the fence of success, were difficult, physically as well as emotionally. After a day's work, my wife would return home to the second job, that of a housewife, to clean, cook and look after the children. As for me, after the office hours, I would be in public libraries, studying books, biographies and "How-to" manuals that were prerequisite for the fruition of our dream. I would come home late and dead-tired. But my wife was always there, waiting for me, to feed me, comfort me, and discuss what we had learned that day and how could they be useful in designing and developing our plan for success.

Hard, and discouraging at times, as those days were, my wife and I often, these days, look back at them where the foolishness, daring and dreams of youth were already laid—unknown and unrecognized—for us, by drawing us together as a compatible and comfortable team, beyond the marital husband-and-wife compatibility. For all purposes of life and living, my wife and I became very successful and satisfying partners. The material successes were not far behind in following.

Before you, dear reader, venture out and take that first step in search of success, whatever that may be, I urge you to seek full partnership with your spouse and with your children, if any. Their support, very often invisible and intangible, is the source of energy and stimulant to feed your determination to succeed.

What good is it if you find success but lose your family or loved ones? Make very sure, your family is there with you every step of the way, to share the bitterness of occasional failures, the strains of weariness and hardship, and finally, to enjoy with you the sweetness of success; it is much more enjoyable that way.

Success, in my book, is the celebration of life to its fullest with the loved ones.

The following pages recount what I have learned and what I have done, with my wife and my family as my partners, in ensuring the prospects and security to celebrate our lives daily.

Follow me.

CHAPTER 4

Investment in real estate?

As I mentioned earlier, a decision has to be based and developed on solid foundation of information, in order to be executed to a successful end.

The necessary information on any decision to invest is available in plenty, and at no cost at all. There are books of all kinds, journals and magazines that deal very extensively with issues such as the decision-making process, how to analyze and adopt a personal choice or preference, how to formulate an initial plan of action, and so on and so forth. These literatures are also available in guide/book style simple language for anyone to follow without help of a university degree or a private tutor. Just check with your nearest public library; you will be pleasantly surprised.

As an accountant by profession, I must admit that I did not give much thought on investments, especially in real estate, untill we bought our first home in Canada. I was puzzled and then impressed by the way right in front of my eyes the property values began to grow, almost overnight, as the new housing community started to take shape and develop into a residential area.

I was intrigued and fascinated by the potential in real estate. I took a few short courses offered by Algonquin College on real estate investment, and I read as much as I could about the business at the public library. And my wife and I made it a ritual every weekend to visit the frantic construction activities in a booming housing market all over Ottawa and surrounding region in the early 1970s.

Why real estate? It somehow does not lend a sexy image, until one reaches the very top, like Campeau or Trump. My own simplistic philosophy on success, as you know now, is very modest. I strongly believe that most people long for, and work hard, to ensure similar modest success. Not all of us are driven or obsessed. Thank God!

The very name real estate, if you think about it, has an overpowering sense and meaning of something real, real in the context of personal estate. Land, as a property, does not vanish and, in the long run, always remain immune to the fluctuations of market speculations. Investment on land may conceivably remain dormant for sometime to react to one or many of the external influences and pressures, like population growth, new economic infrastructure, expansion of human habitat and other stimulants. Less than 25 years ago, in Ottawa, one could buy a house for less than $25,000. Now those houses, old as they are, can, and do, cost anywhere between $100,000 to $200,000, depending upon the areas where they are. You must agree, that is a major appereciation on the initial investment.

That is how real estate appreciates and that is why it is "real" estate. The entire Manhattan Island was bought up for a handful of trinkets and is now worth billions. Less than one hundred years ago, the Americans bought Alaska for a few thousand dollars from the Russians. Now that state is a treasure trove for the U.S. economy.

Compared to other forms of investment and the risks that go more or less with any investment, real estate is relatively safer and more profitable in the long run. Like most ordinary people, in the 1930s my late father bought a life insurance policy to provide for his old age. He kept up the premiums by juggling his limited finances, only to discover following his retirement that he had protection barely for a year! His sacrifice had been for nothing. My father's experience is not unique. It is very common. For people with limited means, like my late father, in real estate investment there is also the satisfaction of building your fortune with your own hands rather than through agents and third parties of various shapes and forms.

By the same token, there is also a guarantee of security in real estate investment. Take the case of my friend in New Jersey. Along with his extensive real estate investments, he was also heavily into the U.S. stock market. Late in 1989, when the bottom dropped from the stock exchanges world wide, my friend, along with millions of investors, lost over $400,000 almost overnight. Unlike many others, he was lucky. His real estate holdings were solid. True, he had to sell most of them to regain his financial footing, but he was saved from a total financial disaster. Real estate is for real.

As for investment capital for that first magic purchase, the size or amount of capital, necessary as it is, is not as important as the knowledge, intimate knowledge of the real estate business. I shall devote an entire later chapter to this important matter of finance.

One thing must be made clear: investment in real estate does not need a lot of guts or audacity as may be needed to go into Futures market. But real estate is very demanding of the investor's dedication, awareness to such changes as demography, zoning, growth of socioeconomic infrastructure, transportation, etc, understanding of the short- and long-term city/municipal plans, and continued efforts to update and increase personal knowledge of real estate.

I suggest that, as a first step, it is a very good idea indeed to sign up for a few weeks' licencing course on real estate with the local community college or real estate board. This not only certifies one to act as a bonafied real estate agent but also gives a chance to make sure that real estate is the thing! Through such a program, you learn about all the rules and regulations pertaining to real estate transaction, the intricacies of financing, and the legal dodahs.

The personal education should also follow through with "free" seminars and "buyers meetings" organized quite frequently by various builders, real estates, local municipal authorities, local chambers or boards of commerce, merchants' associations and community organizations.

All of these are not as difficult or time-consuming as they sound. Do some of them or all of them: use your own judgement. Once you begin, get the hang of things and taste it, you will know intuitively what or how much you are getting and where you are or where you are going.

It is important though that you educate yourself thoroughly so that you can minimize, if not completely eliminate, excess overheads carrying the middlemen, and maximize the intrinsic recognition factor, that is, the full potential for a maximum return on your investment—now as well as in the distant future. Here is another important matter that must be always in front of you: any investment in real estate must have some leeway for an immediate profit, however little or marginal. In fact, I would strongly advise you to buy a property and sell it at market price. This is a starter, a kind of initiation. Even if you make little or no profit, it is o.k., because you taste the excitement and gain experience, which is invaluable. If you just do the buying, you do not complete the cycle of experience without doing some selling as well. Once you have "bloodied" your hands in the full cycle of transaction—and, hopefully, gained an insight into its mystics—you may continue to buy and sell or just buy, depending upon your personal agenda, motivation and resources. However, if you happen to have a lot of money or happen to be a doctor or a lawyer, my own suggestion is that, instead of buying houses, you concentrate on buying tracks of farmland closer to the expanding city limits, the so-called suburbs. And let your property lie there for the inevitable expansion of the city to come to you. Mind you, you will have to pay property taxes. But that is a minor issue. If you wish to recover that cost, well, you may find a few farmers next door to your property willing to rent it from you. On the other hand, if you have no such accommodating neighbor, you may wish to, say, grow radishes there yourself. You may even qualify for some agricultural grants from one or the other level of government.

What I am trying to say is that, like all business ventures, real esatate transactions need insight, intuitive feeling about the property, the location of the property, its character, and all those little things that make a difference but are generally overlooked by many or most of us. You develop a gut feeling, like a sixth sense, by saturating the conscious mind with information, knowledge and expertise about real estate.

It is also worth remembering that wealth acquired by whatever means or modes of business or investment eventually gets diverted and anchored to real estate, giving wealth a permanence and assurance of continued future growth. By the same token, wealth generated through real estate transactions can be, and often is diverted to other, nonreal-estate-based enterprises. But once the wealth is uprooted from real estate, sooner or later; it tends to wither away.

Although real estate demands dedication, it is not demanding; the business can be conducted in the evenings, on weekends, and during holidays. It can be undertaken or conducted from any corner of the earth. And its overheads can be capped and neutralized almost on a permanent basis, depending upon the specific nature of the real estate business. If you are just a buyer-cum-seller, any delay or postponement in the transaction will have no real impact upon your kind of business. On the other hand, a builder or developer of real estate is subject to sudden changes in zoning by-laws, costs of raw materials, changes in labor supply, and changes in weather conditions, among others, that may seriously affect the business and show up in the expected returns on investment.

But, then, that is big-league stuff and does not at the moment concern us. What I am trying to say is that, for an averge person like myself, real estate investment can be safe, fun and profitable venture without being overly exposed to the ups and downs of complex economic influences. People like us do have a job or an occupation to ensure that there is assurance of "bread and butter" for the family table. Any off-time, soft venture, like in real estate transaction, can become the "cherry on the top".

With a little know-how, with a little sense of adventure, and with a little will to do and be better, the cherry can be placed on the top by anyone. I have done it, and, believe me, I am just an ordinary guy.

From here on, why not I take you step by step up the road to success and security that I have been travelling for some twenty-five years?

Follow me!

CHAPTER 5

The measured first step

It must be clear to you by now that determination, conviction and commitment are the preparations for the famous first step to a long journey. The acquisition of knowledge and information is also an integral part of this preparation.

There are, however, some important factors that must not be overlooked. In fact, a fishing expedition without hooks is a tragi-comedy.

Planning is of utmost importance. The planning is the use and utilization of all the factors mentioned for the preparatory stages. It is also an organized, objective and ranked set of steps leading to the goal of success.

Depending upon personal economic or financial circumstances, the following are generally the major planning areas:

(A) Personal security

It is a very good idea indeed to have a job. This provides the security of basic survival. You can ensure the daily bread on the table. It also provides a major backdrop for dealings with financial institutions like banks. We shall discuss this latter leverage in more details further down the road.

(B) Assess personal equity

Surprisingly, most of us have personal worth or equity that we are totally unaware of. If you own a home, it is an asset. What is its present worth? How much can you borrow by using the house as a collateral, if need be? What other durable, cashable assets do you have? Any precious metals and stones? These are some of the hidden assets that need to be catalogued and asked in "money availability" terms. It is also possible, given suffi- cient determination, to start a strict savings schedule, meaning, a strict control over impulsive or compulsive spending on unnecessary or marginal goods and services. For instance, the expensive family holidays or the purchase of a new car can be deferred to a later date. Similarly, such a control will also lead to noticeable shrinkage of the existing debts arising from, among others, excessive use of credit cards.

(C) Internal access to funds

Once you have made a rough assessment of your own current worth, look towards others, such as close family members, relatives and friends, for an assessment of funds available from them as short- or medium-term loan. Once you have convinc- ed them of your business plan, you may be surprised by their willingness to lend you. Never ask for a hand-out: it is a show- stopper.

(D) External sources of funds

The external sources of funds are the conventional banking or financial institutions, such as the places where you do your banking transactions.

For instance, if you bank with ABC Bank or Trust Company or Credit Union or Cooperative, it is a good idea to have a personal meeting with the Branch Manager to discuss your standing with the institution, your credit worthiness, your immediate business plans and financial requirements. It is quite possible that your plans will receive an understanding hearing, that your credit ratings are quite high and that you are in a position to receive a larger loan than you ever expected, based only on your job as a collateral.

This is a scenario true for most individuals. Let me tell you about my son: after graduation from the University, he decided to go into real estate investment. Although I was ready to help him get started, he decided to do it on his own. He went to his bank to establish a line of credit. He borrowed $25,000 and paid back the entire loan within one month through his first transaction in real estate—a house. Because of his promptness in repaying the loan, within 6 months, the bank increased his line of credit to $50,000 and, again, to $75,000, without requiring any security or any request from my son. In order to strengthen further this credit worthiness, you may wish to borrow, even if you do not need it, say $500 for, say, two months and then repay it within one month. This enhances your image as a good customer with the bank and enables you to borrow yet again a larger sum of money, to repeat the same process. You only need to repeat the process a few times. You will be surprised by the increase in confidence in your credit ratings, which, in turn, will enable you to borrow a much larger sum of money without any problem for later business needs. The important thing about this operation is that it makes you a friend and trusted customer of the banking house and makes the latter a willing silent partner in your business venture who does not share in your future profits.

As much as you want trusting friends in your banking institution, it is good to remember that you too must make a commitment to do business with that institution as your business venture matures and prospers. That way, your growth will bring business to the banking house, it will establish further your standing and improve your credibility for larger and larger financial support for future dealings.

You may wonder, if this is so simple, why others are not doing it? Well, one answer is that most people do not have the dedicated commitment to a single objective. The financial institutions, in the very first meeting with the prospective borrower, looks for that commitment along with things like collaterals and the capacity to pay. Have you ever wondered why thousands of dollars are given out as mortgages or as car loans to so many, so easily? Because they have the confidence in the real estate or the car that is being purchased.

You build on that confidence. Once you have demonstrated that the money lent to you is not only safe but is also being productive and profitable, you have more or less a free licence to come and borrow as much as you wish.

Now that the money business has been taken care of, you must turn attention to the business proper, buying real estate.

Here again, you will be wise not to run out and buy the first house or property you see. You must plan your first buy most carefully and do such planning during all other future transactions.

(E) **Planning the first buy**

The important thing is that you have to cultivate faith in yourself. You have to take your courage in your hands and jump in. As a boy, when I went to learn swimming, I was scared at first. I spent a lot of time just sitting beside the pool, watching other swimmers. I spent a lot more time just wading in the shallow waters. My instructor tried to encourage me about the improbability of drowning if I had the will to swim. Well, to make it short, finally, he dumped me in the deeper waters. I panicked, I spluttered and I kicked wildly in the water. But then lo and behold, I was not drowning. I was swimming, well, not like an Olympic athlete, but I was swimming. I am sure, most of us learn to swim more or less in this fashion.

Faith, courage and desire to survive, panic notwithstanding, do the trick. And so it is also with real estate investment or any other endeavor in life.

The first thing to do is to get a map of your town or city. Mark out the areas where new constructions are taking place, the established residential areas, and the commercial areas. The second step is to decide whether you want to concentrate in residential or commercial properties. In residential properties, you may wish to decide upon new properties or older, in-need-of-repair properties.

Let us have a quick look at the various aspects of each of these options.

Residential properties, new and old, like the commercial properties can change hands easily. The only difference is that a commercial property needs a much larger capital outlay. For instance, if you wish to buy up an entire apartment building, you are looking at a large down payment. The arrangement of mortgages will depend upon the location of the building, the vacancy rates, and such other relevant and important matters. Much the same situation will also face a decision to buy a shopping mall or a commercial building.

In case of new residential buildings, you may be able to make some arrangements with the builder as regards the down payments as well as mortgages. However, it is good to remember that depending upon the location of the new property and the general economic conditions, especially the going mortgage rates, the appreciation in value between the buying and selling the property may not be very high. This is because, (i) you have to pay the prevalent or the going inflated price to the builder when buying, (ii) you will have to compete with the builder's offered price when selling, and (iii) the extras thrown in as bonus by the builder to prospective customers to cushion even higher prices may work against your profit margin.

The best deal, in my own experience is to aim for smaller and/or older homes. In Houston, Texas, my friend Mr. Shah was busy buying expensive, big houses. He reasoned that the property prices would continue to rise and, as a result, with each sale, he would make more than marginal profit. In the meantime, as rental units, these high-class, high-priced houses would attract the rich tenants. He was wrong on all counts. With the oil price bust, Texas, like every other oil country, had to buckle down on extravagance. The big, expensive properties do not move as easily as any other smaller- or medium-sized properties. Only the rich can afford either to buy or rent them and the rich do such things less frequently. Above all, for every rich person, there are at least 1000 average persons, who are the real economic forces that all businesses compete to capture. My friend's strategy failed and left him stranded on the verge of financial ruin.

On the other hand, take the case of a friend of mine who, on retirement from Canadian Armed Forces, asked me how he could use his time and a part of his savings in real estate. My first advise to him was to take a short course on real estate, to study the market in town and, then, to make his first investment on a modest scale. He did all of that. Over time, he began to specialize in low- to medium-priced houses, where, at least in Ottawa, there is always a quick and reasonably good market. Today, he is no longer a moderately comfortable retiree. He is a millionaire—and he did achieve this spectacular success after his retirement! The advantages are: (i) houses are settled and established with landscaping, etc.; (ii) the existing mortgages may well be reasonably large, at a lower rate and perfectly transferable; (iii) the vendor may be willing to take a second mortgage at a rate lower than the going one; and (iv) some additional extension, addition, or repair and repainting job substantially increase the property value right off the bat. It has been my experience that dealing with such properties you can, if wished, make a quick profit of a couple of thousand dollars even as you finalize and close the deal. My father used to say that even a fool can make some profit in real estate. To that

I can add my own experience and say that this profit can be increased a lot, I mean, a lot, if the fool can wait and hold off selling for ten to fifteen years. During this time, all properties experience a natural rate of appreciation in value.

Well, enough said on this. Let us now look at what to do with the map you have already marked out.

Once you have decided on your choice of residential or commercial properties, start a thorough examination of the officially planned growth considerations for your town or city and its immediate environment, the plans for major residential, commercial construction drives, and the plans for social infrastructure, like schools, hydro, sanitation, road system, and hundred-and-one other essentials that make our lives comfortable. You may wish to go down to the City Hall and get the "free" copies of their present and future plans and intentions; talk to the public officials and the city counsellors. I found out in 1989, that Nepean, a sister city to Ottawa, has a plan already in the works to expand the city's population to 100,000 by 1995. To this end, lands have already been "cleared" in the north, northwest of Barrhaven, the commercial areas, complete with an industrial park, have been designated and the blueprints for residential construction are being readied for builders. Now, this kind of information is worth the weight in gold for investors who can plan their acquisition well ahead of the actual event.

The other thing that you as investor must explore is the going or current prices for properties that are your target. Take a city or townwide view. Be a statistician. Catalogue the prices of, say, single houses, bungalows, or whatever in the east end, west end, center of city, etc., and compare them. This is very important.

For example, a two-storey, 4-bedroom house or a duplex in center town will be priced different from a similar one in east or west end of the town. There will also be considerable price difference between east and west end of the town. There are many peculiar variations, causes and rationales for such variations. I cannot give a simple explanation to clear away the causes; but I can assure you, that once you begin to explore and examine your city or town, you will get to know the differences and their economic, social and psychological substances.

Once this overall orientation or ground work is done, choose a growth area—an area where the future growth is planned for. Difficult as it may sound, it is, in reality, easier to make such a choice. As mentioned before, go to your City Hall, talk to the officials, the local politicians because such plans are for public use. You may also talk to the area's financial institutions, the business people, the Chamber of Commerce, the Board of Trade, and the community organizations as well as some area lawyers. And, before you know, you will have more information than you can use. There is also a secondary benefit of such personal contacts—you establish a human as well as potential business relation that may come in handy at some future time.

You may also look closely around the neighborhood of your workplace. The advantages of a home or investment close to where you work, are many—and you know it. A few years ago, a doctor friend of mine moved to Ottawa from London, England, with his wife. He was living in a rented apartment close to where he practiced. One day he saw a big, older home up for sale within walking distance from his office. He liked the house, the location and the advantage of being close to his practice. The asking price was about $95,000. He was not sure if that was a wise decision to make at that time. He came to see me. We examined the pros and cons. It came down to this: my friend had no children, so why buy a big house? He also did not have the down payment, so why make the investment? On the other hand, he realized that, as a doctor, he would have a larger future income and that eventually he would have children as well. Above all, the location was excellent and the investment would not sour. So, we went and had another look at the property. We also negotiated the selling price down to about $87,000. I persuaded my friend to buy the house with the guarantee that if he did not like or feel comfortable with this decision at the end of 3 years, I would buy it from him at his purchase price. Well, now he has two children; so, he needs all the space. The market value of his property has gone up to some $450,000 according to the last count. And, I do not have his house. He has it!

Once you have analyzed and settled on a specific area where you wish to do business, I suggest that you clearly mark out a few square miles of that chosen area. Let us call it your target area. Now, you begin in earnest to study your target area as intimately as possible. Find out and know all there is to know about your target area, about things like the quality of schools, quality of transportation, the general socioeconomic status of the people, the tax rates, the nature and incidences of crime, to name but a few. You will have to talk to the householders, businesses and institutions in your target area. You will know the area like the back of your hand. Once you have done that, you are ready.

But, wait! Ready you may be, but do you know when to make a deal to buy? You do know, of course, that buy when it is a buyer's market, that is, when you can pick and choose and make any offer dictated by your own capacity. In Canada, winter is such a time. Properties for sale during winter generally means that the vendor is under some pressure to sell. Winter dictates lower than standard value of the property and there are also fewer likely prospective buyers. At such times, you may, what am I saying, you will be able to strike a better bargain in terms of final selling price, closing time, mortgage negotiations and occupancy.

Heartless as it may sound, when the mortgage rates are high and soaring, a lot of householders are forced to sell their properties. Under such circumstances, the selling prices are invariably lower than the property value and the owners are under some pressure to unload their properties. A potential buyer can do well taking advantage of the misfortunes of others caught in the mortgage squeeze.

It is also important that you remain close to, and in constant touch with, where your action is. Some years ago, a friend of mine became interested in real estate investment in the West Coast of Canada. It was oil-boom time and Calgary was attracting lots of people like my friend. He dispatched his son to supervise the action. The son went off to Calgary and in no time acquired three properties. Then, instead of staying close to his investment, he returned to Ottawa. The properties were rented out but the control was lost. To make the long story short, when the boom phased out, there was no one on hand to look after this little investment. The opportunity was lost and so was the profit.

It is good to remember that, once you own properties, the better time of selling is when it is a seller's market, that is, when there are more buyers than sellers. In Canada, if winter is the buyer's market, the spring and summer are the seller's market; this is the time when prospective buyers are looking for homes to buy, are moving to new areas, etc. It is also worth remembering that when the mortgage rates are lower, people are more serious about buying and, in consequence, the house prices tend to go up higher and that is definitely to the advantage of the seller.

I did mention earlier that if you happen to be handy with tools, a few hundred dollars worth of addition or additional work on the house can easily add a few extra thousand dollars to the selling price.

It is also good to remember what once Howard Hughes said about striking rich: Do the opposite of what others are doing and you will eventually benefit. I like to add my own bit of wisdom to it: Have patience, give some time, and it will mean money in the bank.

Before closing this chapter, let us recapitulate what we must emphasize for a first-time buyer or any entrepreneur in real estate:

(1) Plan, gather information.
(2) Get to know the people, the local politicians, the civic authorities, community organizations, business community, the professionals like areas doctors, lawyers, bankers, etc.
(3) Study your town or city: collect and compare the areas for growth, prices, etc.
(4) Select a specific area as your target area, no more than a few square miles in radius, to get to know intimately before beginning operation almost exclusively at the beginning stages.
(5) Take stock of your own financial status.
(6) Explore sources of funds and/or short-term soft loans from among relatives, close friends and associates.
(7) Visit your banking house and establish personal contact and get an idea of your eligibility for loans.
(8) Work out a plan to establish financial credibility and credit worthiness.

CHAPTER 6

Buying first property: the great search

Buying a property, for personal residence or investment, is the same thing in the long run: it is an investment into the future. Because of this, unlike any other form of investment, a decision to invest on a real estate property calls for a vision not only of what one needs now and will need, say, 10 or 15 years from now, a vision of what the neighborhood may look like in the future, and a vision of what the economic impact will be on the investment in some distant future.

If you have thoroughly studied the real estate market in general, and your target area in particular, and if you have boned up on the local developments put up by the different levels of government, and if you have analyzed all these bits of information carefully before making the decision to buy that most important first buy, I should say, you are as ready as ever likely to be.

But, wait! Don't just run out there and make an offer to buy the first house for sale in your target area! Go out to your target area, scout around and locate the properties offered for sale. Get hold of their asking prices, the details of each of these properties and the premises, make note of the most noticeable, least cost, most visually effective improvements that may be made to add to the resale value, make note of the condition and quality of the neighborhood of each of the offered properties.

Now go on to the next, more important, bottom line calculations of your gains on each of the properties. Simply make out a detailed income-expenditure table for each to determine the monthly and yearly operating or running expenses against the revenues and make out a rough estimate of the total costs and revenues for income tax purposes (See the attached form, Appendix D, p. 106). Don't worry if your net gains show up a little in the red. It will look rosy in your income tax returns.

Once you have made up the comparative rough expenditure-revenue tables for each of the prospective properties on sale in your target area, make out the initial bid and final offer to purchase on each, reflecting the margin of profit shown in your expenditure-revenue tables. Now you are ready.

Go out there, and make the initial, starting offer to each of the properties. Make sure, your initial offer is reasonably (or, even unreasonably!) low. The other thing to remember is that you ought to concentrate first on those properties that are already vacated. A vacant property means that the owner has already moved, for one reason or another, and is under some pressure to get the property off his hands in a hurry. The chances are that a favorably good deal you can have.

Although, in most instances, the properties for sale are listed with a real estate agent, the real seller is just one step behind. Make a low offer through the listing agent and, then, request that you would like to negotiate the final price as well as the conditions of sale with the vendor, the owner. His broker, the real estate agent, does not play the game of 'offers and counter offers' without the full approval of the vendor, whose needs and priorities ultimately determine the final price and the conditions of sale, subject, of course, to the legal adviser of the buyer and the seller. In other words, try to reach the vendor early in the game and try to deal with him as directly as possible.

On the aside, it is good to remember that dealing with properties on sale by owner or vendor are likely to be price adjusted for the 5–7% fees of the real estate agent. The vendor will also be more amenable to other important concessions and adjustments in the selling price. He may, for instance, be persuaded to leave the tracks and/or the curtains in the house; the washer, dryer, fridge may also be included in the deal.

It is a good idea to make sure if the existing mortgage on the property, depending upon the rate and volume as well as on the coverage time, is transferable. Most vendors are willing and prepared to take a second mortgage, at a lower than going rate and for a shorter time, say one or two years, because such a course of action helps unload the property and offers some extra revenue to the vendor.

A good business practice is to find a good lawyer, one whom you can trust and be on friendly terms, so that you can call on his counsel whenever needed. Such a lawyer need not be on retainers like the story-book wheelers and dealers do. You can pay as you go—on a case by case basis. Just call a handful of local lawyers, preferably those who are younger and new in business, in your neighborhood and check out their consulting fees schedules. Select the one you like and think you can live with. A prospect of steady, continuing and growing business relation will tempt an aspiring lawyer to offer his services at reasonable costs per shot.

Let this lawyer work out the details and the paper works for closing the final deal and the transfer and possession of the property.

Now is the time you must make a final decision on what you want to do with the property you have become the owner of. If it is for rental purposes, then it is a good idea to start looking for someone to rent to, even before the key to the property is in your hand. The way to go about it is to put up an advertisement in the local newspaper's 'For Rent' sections; you may wish to, with the approval of the vendor, put up a "For Rent" sign on the property's lawn, or pin similar signs on the bill boards of local stores. None of these, except the newspaper ad, costs any money. And then, there is the grapevine of word of mouth among friends, colleagues and acquaintances to locate a prospective client.

If you are renting, make sure that, if nothing else, the rent covers the monthly mortgage costs. Even on a break-even situation you will be ahead in the game. If there is a short fall, you may not be in trouble immediately, but watch out!

However, if you want to sell it off right away, you may put an ad in your local newspaper to that effect. You may wish to do so without a real estate agent. If so, put up an appropriate lawn sign as well. My own recommendation is not to put the property up for sale immediately. You see, depending upon the market conditions, you may stand to gain very little, if at all. From the time you buy the property and turn around to sell it within a few days or weeks, the market conditions are not likely to change so dramatically as to generate any profit at all. Some years ago, an economist friend became very interested, and in retrospect, very anxious, to become a real estate tycoon in a big hurry. He came to me for advice. It appeared that he had the ambition but no concrete plans and, of course, no idea as to where the monies for the down payment, etc., would come from. As we talked, it became clear that he expected me to take care of these small problems by selling a few of my holdings to him at no down payment. Since he was a friend and had a good federal government job, I decided to help him out and "sold" him four houses. This gentleman, an economist, was more interested in turning around and putting up these properties for sale after he discovered that investment in real estate needed some dedication and care, not to mention some attention to proper upkeeps and management. In his hurry, he failed to rent out these properties, which meant a net loss and a heavy pressure to meet the mortgage commitments. I saw him struggle to sell them off at outlandish asking prices. You see, he was determined to make it rich without really trying. Well, he struggled for a couple of years, almost to the point of financial calamity. Then he came back to me complaining that I had sold him some duds—unsellable properties, and asked that I take them off his hands. I was glad to do this favor to my friend. After taking them back, I had no difficulty to make them pay their way. My prescription is simple: Patience and time add up to money, lots of it.

Following this home-grown, well-tested prescription, you take possession of the property; spend some time taking notes and making assessment of the possible repairs and/or renovations to the property that you can, with the help of your friends and family members, undertake at very little costs and efforts; also any major jobs to be given out to contractors. Keep in mind, all of these are to increase the quality of the property, which, in turn, will substantially increase the selling price. If any renovation or repair job has to be given to a contractor, talk to as many contractors as possible, have them come over to examine the job to be done. Once you have selected a contractor, organize a mutually satisfactory work schedule and costs.

If the property is not yet in your possession but a deal has been struck, make the renovation/repair job a part of the deal so that the work can go on and coincide with the actual closing of the deal as closely as possible. The main advantage here is that you take possession of already vastly more valuable property without paying for it. It is also possible that the vendor may be put in an awkward position, psychologically speaking, for the "miserable state" of his property, and. thus, be easily persuaded to fork up at least a part, if not the whole, of the repair/renovation costs.

And take advantage of this situation irrespective of whether you wish to rent the property or just turn around and put it back on market for sale.

Rent or sell, you now have a property. Congratulations! We shall recapitulate the important steps: first acquisition and then move on to some more important matters.

The important steps to remember are:

(1) Make note of all (or as many as possible) properties up for sale in the target area. Establish the market value for each of these properties. Make note of their asking prices as well as the possible selling prices.

(2) Make note of the vendors /real estate agents.

(3) See each of the properties and get the following information:

    (a) the asking prices;

    (b) the details on the conditions of transaction (see the attached list for conditions, Appendix C, p. 101–105);

    (c) Mortgage information, e.g., outstanding amounts, rates, with whom, how long to renewal, transferability, etc.;

    (d) condition of property on premises as well as on the property, i.e., front and back yards;

    (e) need for repair/renovation, etc.;

    (f) miscellaneous, e.g., what all is included in the asking price.

(4) Make up a chart or table listing the operating costs and the likely revenues on each of the properties. This will give you an idea of how much money you can put out (see the attached form, Appendix D, p. 106).

(5) Find out why the property is for sale.

(6) Find out whether the vendor is willing to take second mortgage.

(7) Find out the possible occupancy date.

(8) Try to establish personal contact with the vendor.

(9) Make a low offer and work up to your price.

(10) Assess the vendor's real need and price before making your final offer.

(11) Select a young, but efficient, lawyer to work for you on regular basis and have him organize the final stage of negotiations and the closing of the deal.

(12) Sell or rent, try, with the approval of the vendor, to undertake any least-cost but financially rewarding repairs and/or renovations before the final closing of the deal.

CHAPTER 7

Financing: where is the down payment?

It is a very good idea to keep track of your financial abilities, availabilities and liabilities at all times. It is also especially important when you are out shopping for properties.

As you make ready for the first purchase, as you know, your offer is accompanied with a cheque of $1,000.00 or more, depending upon the asking price. This is a sign of good intent. When the final price is agreed upon and the deal is made, this initial offer is included in the final settlement. The final settlement is, however, made when you make the agreed and conventional down payment of 20%–25% of the final and the mutually agreed price. This cheque is held in escrow by your lawyer.

The balance of the monies has to be raised through mortgage vendors like banks, trust companies and private sources. Before going to any one of these, it is important to explore whether there is any substantial mortgage on the property, its time of expiry and renewal and its interest rates as well as the prospects and conditions for reassumption by a new owner. The possibility that the vendor may be willing to assume a second mortgage is also important. The amount of second mortgage and the interest rate to be changed by the vendor should be looked into. You may have to work a little hard to persuade the vendor, since your ultimate objective is to put the minimum acceptable down payment. Once these have been looked after, away you go to your friendly banker (the mortgage department) and apply for either renewal of the existing mortgage or a new one. The mortgage department has all the necessary forms with them. You will be required to provide full and detailed information on your financial status, that is, your income (including that of the wife, if she is working), your standard expenses, your debts (including those outstanding on credit cards), the name(s) of your places of banking, your other assets and that includes your currently owned house or a place of residence. Depending upon the viability of these bits of information and the amount of mortgage you are asking for (which, incidentally, according to Canada Mortgage and Housing Corporation (CMHC) regulations, may not exceed 40% tops of your gross income), the Mortgage Department will procure a report from the appraiser (of the bank) on the real worth of the designated property. If everything goes as it should, you will be advised of the approval, generally within 5–7 days from application.

If the vendor is unwilling to take a second mortgage under any circumstances, then you will have to go to finance or trust companies or to private investors through lawyers. You must, under these conditions, try to secure a second mortgage for the longest period possible. Under no circumstances should you take out a short-term (that is, 6–12-month) second mortgage. Also you must "try" to strike a deal that leaves the contract open for earlier retirement of obligations without any penalty.

On the other hand, if the vendor is willing to give you a second mortgage, but his own mortgage on the property you are buying is very small, you can try to convince him, before the conclusion of the deal, to refinance his old mortgage up to 90%–95% of the value and keep the money, while you simply take over the obligations of making payments to the mortgage. That way, the vendor stands to gain all the legal and refinancing costs that you pay to him directly.

The beauty of the underlying reason lies in its simplicity: you as a buyer can command, by law, only up to 75% of the property value, especially if you are an investor, whereas the vendor as the owner-occupant can get a much higher ratio mortgage—up to 90%—in refinancing the existing mortgage.

The other alternative, as mentioned earlier, is to seek financing from private sources. For this, you will have to contact lawyers, including your own. Private lenders generally go into such operations through lawyers. Be prepared, however, to pay much higher interest rates, higher than even the conventional second mortgage rates.

A mortgage broker is yet another source for second mortgages. This source arranges mortgages for a fixed or negotiated fee payable for personal services, in addition to the standard fees.

There are, of course, always the friends, relatives and members of your personal inner circle, who may either individually or collectively put together a package of second mortgage money for a negotiated period of time. Being of personal nature, the details are likely to vary from person to person. Just make one thing clear: let it be properly business-like. That way you can save your own face as well as your friendship.

Personally, I strongly believe that it is advisable to borrow from financial institutions. There are many obvious advantages. For instance, in case you need to renew your second mortgage, you can negotiate the new contract at the prevailing market rate of interest, a thing that may not be possible either with private investor or with members of your personal inner circle.

It is, of course, preferable if you do not need to finance your first operation through any form of second or third mortgage. If you need such a financing, try and make sure that this becomes due at the same time as your first mortgage. This way, not only do you have a better grasp of your liabilities, you can also, if you wish to, or need to, refinance the existing first and second mortgages for a higher-volume first mortgage only. The monkey of a second mortgage will be off your back. Even with a higher first mortgage rate, your total cost of borrowing will be lower than carrying two mortgages.

Now that we have looked into the sources of money, let us sum up the important points for easy reference:

(1) For down payment, try to pull as much as you can from your personal resources, friends, relatives and close associates.

(2) Vendor renews his existing mortgage (at your costs) and transfers to you.

(3) Vendor takes a second mortgage.

(4) Contact your bank for first mortgage.

(5) The private investors through lawyers are another source of financing, though most expensive.

(6) Mortgage brokers, for personal services fees, locate and arrange financing.

(7) Due date for first and all other mortgages should preferably fall at the same time.

(8) While refinancing, roll back the second mortgage with higher-volume first mortgage.

(9) Should you need a second mortgage, do not take a short-term loan of 6–12 months duration; make it as long-term as possible, with the option for earlier retirement of all or part of such mortgages.

CHAPTER 8

Mortgages and their creative uses

Let me begin this chapter by telling you how I recently made a significant real estate acquisition in Ottawa. This commercial/office building is located in the hub of a commercial area. The owner of the property was a major bank. The sale sign was on for a long time. I was interested and puzzled by the situation: Why was the property not moving? From the real estate agents I learned that the property was for sale at $1.3 million, then at $1.1 million. No dice. The bank was losing some $250,000 (if they had been paying normal mortgage payments) each year and had, in fact, lost some $1.0 million during the past 4 years.

Clearly, the owner—the bank—was in a dilemma. When I, along with my wife and brother, decided to make a bid, the property was taken off the market. No matter, I contacted the bank's Toronto office and made an all-cash offer of $750,000. The bank made a counter offer of $800,000 but it finally accepted original $750,000 cash offer.

I needed to raise funds. My banks were reluctant to give me mortgage on this property. Well, I did not share their concern about the wisdom of buying the property where one of their own was losing money. I convinced the mortgage companies holding mortgages on my other properties to hold them as securities against approximately $560,000. For the rest, I managed to take out second mortgages with other companies.

I bought this commercial/office building for $750,000. It is all rented out and as of now, the assessed market value of the property is now over $4 million. I expect that within a few years, it may be worth over $6 million.

Mortgage is the fancy name of borrowing money to buy a real estate property. So long as the borrower—the mortgagor—pays up his loan, he has the ownership and the possession of the property.

Access to mortgage money is important for playing the real estate game. This is true for a millionaire as well as a middle income earner, because the necessary cash is available without liquidating any assets. Mortgages also give the necessary flexibility in moving in and out of deals on a very short notice.

There are risks involved, as to be expected. If the regular—usually monthly—payments are defaulted for a time beyond stipulated, the property in question may be seized by the mortgagee—the lender—and be disposed off to recover the monies lent. This is not an unusual situation, but it happens rather infrequently. As you may or may not know, in Canada or in the United States, over 90% of the properties owned are financed through mortgages.

Since mortgage involves a cost, it is the interest rate that makes mortgages rather expensive. In order to have a "clear" ownership of your property, say 25 years from the date of purchase, your property value, that is, the total price will be the selling price that you negotiated at the time of purchase (which includes also the total amount of mortgage you have taken out), plus the total amount that you have paid out as interest on the mortgage amount over the 25-year period.

The initial value of the property is substantially lower than the total subsequent payments to the mortgage.

It may all sound somewhat complicated; in fact, it is a complex matter, but there is simplicity in it as well, which is the key to the ritual of mortgage lending.

You may recall that I have tried to emphasize that knowledge and a lot of it is most important in any venture. As you begin to prepare intellectually and psychologically to get into real estate investment, you should have talks with your banker. Ask him to explain how "you", under various imaginary financial situation, can apply for mortgages. The banker will be glad to be your tutor and provide you with the knowledge of the financial institutions' for the ever-continuing love affair with real estate and with those who wish to acquire real estate. By the same token, you should also talk to real estate agents. These are the people who really play the two ends against (or in favor of) the middle. What they do not know about the ins and outs of mortgage financing are not worth bothering about. Go and visit as many "Open Houses" as you possibly can.

In any case, it is good to know that real estate attracts mortgage monies, unless there is something really nasty larking underneath. Indeed, a given real estate can have one, two, or more mortgages against it. As to be expected, in case of default by the mortgagor, the right to recovery rests first with the first mortgage holder, and there on down the line. You can understand why the interest rates on second, third, etc., mortgages are substantially higher than those on the first mortgage.

This is a sort of reward for taking a greater degree of risk. If, for instance, the defaulted property falls short of meeting the liabilities of the first mortgage upon liquidation, the mortgage holder down the line is going to be out of luck. Similarly, if the last mortgage holder wishes to foreclose a property, he must be prepared to pay off the lenders ahead of him.

Because of this built-in risk factor, by government regulation, the first mortgage may not exceed beyond a certain predetermined proportion of the property value. In Canada, it is 75% although there are instances where it is reasonably flexible. In the United States, where the system is somewhat different in matters of assessing a potential mortgagor, the proportion can go as high as 90%. There is no such limit imposed on second or successive mortgages—although the market value and the mortgagor's credit worthiness play a significant role in setting the maximum limit.

There are different kinds of mortgages. Let us look briefly at some of the most popular ones.

In general, one may wish to consider a mortgage loan on fixed rate or floating rate. For obvious reasons, a floating rate is just what it means, it fluctuates from day to day, responding to various market forces and conditions. In the long run, one is liable to pay a high rate of interest more often than a lower one, at least in the lifetime of the particular deal, and may end up paying very high indeed. On the other hand, a fixed rate is like a relatively stable rock in a fluctuating water line. One locks up against a given prevailing rate, for the required duration. There are, of course, certain risks. For instance, a deal may be closed for five to twenty-five years at a rate that may just come down a notch or more a few days later. With no way to break the agreement or contract without paying substantial penalty, some psychological discontent may have to be faced, although in money terms, no big loss is experienced. It must be remembered that interest rates do fluctuate and are never fixed in the market place, unless they are locked-in under specific deals. And there are more upward, violently upward, swings in interest rates than there are dramatically downward slides.

Normally, standard first mortgages are offered for a five-year period, with amortization varying 20–25 years. It is not advisable to seek or accept mortgages for less than 5 years if the current interest rates are not very high. This offers a reasonable security against loss of property due to some drastic change in the money market or in the overall economic conditions, like a barn burner inflation or a severe depression. Remember the gruesome tales of the Depression of 1929.

It stands to reason that if you are assuming the existing mortgage on the property you are buying, you have got the simplest of all deals—provided it has at least a few more years to go. If, on the other hand, the existing mortgage has less than a year to go, you may do well to try and negotiate with the vendor to increase the mortgage for full five years. Naturally, the same holds true if the mortgage is held by a financial institution.

On the aside, election years, especially in the United States, are the best of times to make a better deal on mortgages and the accompanying interest rates. The money is more plentiful and the interest rates are, historically, lower, no matter what the general economic forecasts.

The interest-only mortgage is not a common garden variety mortgage. Nonetheless, it is there, usually obtainable from a wealthy relative—the in-laws perhaps! But, if you are a skilled negotiator, it is possible to get such mortgage from the vendor or even a financial institution. This mortgage plan helps keep your cash flow at some respectable level. You just pay the accruing interests while the real value of the borrowed principal tends to decline. At the end of contractual term, the entire principal becomes due, payable by cash (!) or with new financing.

Yet another interesting idea in mortgage market involves plans for graduated payments: the payments start on the low side and accelerate at some higher rate over the entire term of the contract, reaching a crescendo at the end. It can begin with a lot of variation, for example, begin with payment of interest only, graduate to interest plus certain portion of the principal, and so on, reflecting (hopefully) increases in income flow. The only good thing about this scheme is that, for the duration, the interest rate remains fixed.

There are other types of mortgages, like the wrap-around mortgage, which means negotiation of a new mortgage including the existing mortgage on a property, presumably in the hope that the average of lower interest rate on the existing mortgage and the higher interest rate on the new mortgage will be relatively lower than the stand-alone rate on new mortgage.

Or, a blanket mortgage that covers more than one property owned by a single mortgagor. Such a mortgage is generally for large real estate developers and corporate builders, and hardly ever available for a single-unit (or multiple-unit) property owner. And then, there is the vendor take-back kind, that, under ordinary circumstances, may be termed as the best kind. This form of mortgage leaves ample room for creative negotiations with the vendor, thus saving a considerable amount of monies and head-aches for the buyer. The vendor too, comes far better off.

The vendor simply allows the buyer to continue to owe money after the conclusion of the deal. The existing mortgage is transferred or renegotiated by the vendor or simply sold to a mortgage broker. Such deals are often made by offering the vendor attractive bonus, or by offering to pay higher interest rates instead of lower payments through lower purchase price or some adjustments in amortization.

We now reach a point where one needs to ask whether it is wise to assume or take over an existing mortgage. Well, the answer is simple really. It is strictly subject to the original agreements and/or conditions set out when the mortgage was first negotiated by the mortgagor and the mortgagee. If it is o.k. there, the second step is to look at the amount of mortgage remaining, the balance of the time (average) remaining, and, importantly, the rate of interest applicable. If, on all these scores the answer is favorable (in the context of the prevailing conditions), then, by all means, go ahead and take it over.

There is a not so major point outstanding in our discussion so far. What kind of amortization period to look for? Amortization simply means that the monthly payment of a mortgaged property is a sum of portions of the principal and the interest which is calculated and paid each month on the outstanding balance. Over time, as the amount of mortgage decreases, the payments on the principal increase and those on the interest decrease. That is why your payments for the first few years—usually about 5 years—contain very little of the principal and are reflective entirely of interest payments. Similarly, at the tail end, you pay off a lot—if not most—of the principal.

As I mentioned earlier, in Canada, the most common and preferred amortization period is 25 years. Although the term is usually for 5 years, the calculation of interest payments and the pay-off time is based on 25 years. At the time of renewal (at the end of 5 years), one may negotiate a shorter amortization period, keeping in mind though that you may have to make larger monthly payments.

Unless one has access to larger cash flows, the shorter amortization period and, therefore, larger monthly payments can be a bit of a problem. On the other hand, a shortening of this period, say from 25 to 20 years, does nothing positive either for your cash flow situation or for the value of the property.

A longer amortization period is perhaps the best way to go, for the rich as well as the not-so-rich (yet!) owner.

The financing of ownership of a property is as much a matter of one's financial resources as it is of one's creative negotiating skill. While it is almost impossible to borrow necessary capital without any interest payments (unless it is a simple one-cent transfer from parents or relatives), it is possible to look deep and hard into the causes and problems facing the vendor. Try out some of the creative solutions that may lighten a vendor's burden of immediate problems and you may negotiate with him some uniquely advantageous real estate transactions.

You may, for instance, negotiate lower or even differed down payment, giving you enough time to organize your specific plans for the property. Or, you may negotiate with the vendor a mortgage, split into first, second, even a third, at different rates of interests applicable to each. Just so long you do not cut down the total gains of the vendor, and just so long the vendor can live with any combination in a deal, you try to maximize your benefits on all fronts.

And then there are ways, perhaps not too conventional, whereby you may try to reduce or even eliminate the need for larger mortgages.

One of the generally successful way is to locate a property in a "growth area" and then, instead of negotiation for a lower price on the property, focus on a low down payment while offering to pay the asking price. Some say that the psychology of the strategy is such that the vendor is bowled over by such turn of events and is prepared even to take a reasonable chunk of mortgage on market rate of interest.

Anything is possible!

On the other hand, as I mentioned earlier if a vendor can be persuaded to take out a new mortgage on the property before the transaction, and, at the same time, is also willing to assume a second mortgage at a lower rate, then the new buyer has done himself well!

CHAPTER 9

Strategic decisions on buying & selling

Before you go into real estate business, it is important that you have some clear idea about what you intend to do with the properties you buy. You must know that wanting to make money is only the goal, not the answer. There is a major decision area between the acquisition of property and money-making.

In order to make money—to make a profit is a better description—you have to sell the property that you have bought. When to sell it is the question, and a decision that must be made with some deliberate calculation. This calculation must be based on the knowledge of the market.

You remember what I said about buying when it is a buyer's market. This buyer's market is simply not going to vanish as soon as you have done with your buying. So, you cannot just turn around and put up a sale sign on your property. Well, you can, but you are then a part of the buyer's market, you cannot expect to dominate the price, the buyer will. You will have to wait for the market to come around to the seller's market condition, when there are not too many houses up for sale and when, as a seller, you can control the selling price.

Some years ago, a friend decided a leave a lucrative medical practice and go into real estate investment in Ottawa. It was a time when Ottawa was going through a residential construction boom, especially in condominium units. My friend, as a doctor, had no difficulty in opening up a fair access to mortgage funds; he also had a respectable bank balance to go into the market in a real big way. As he studied the Ottawa housing market, he realized that the big construction spree on condo units was creating a major demand slack through oversupply of condos. Lo and behold, even as he was getting ready to test the market, his diagnosis turned out to be true. There was a buyer's market in Ottawa's condo units. In fact, it was a bargain-hunter's dream. My friend bought over 300 condo units. They are all rented and return a fair profit for the owner. The market value of these units, well, let me not guess!

Although I did not take advantage of this condo bonanza (don't ask me why), my brother did. He too bought a fair number of these units and has been doing extremely well since then in his real estate deals and, of course, in his personal finances.

What all these suggest is that a study of the market and patience combine to give one the foresight needed in succeeding in business.

In other words, again, knowledge of the market and patience are the two major conditions you must satisfy.

My own experience suggests that once you have purchased a property, you undertake some real and cosmetic repair and renovation job on the property. Rent it out at a price that guarantees, at the very least, the coverage of monthly mortgage payments, assuming that the tenant pays for all utilities and assuming that all taxes on the property are included in the monthly mortgage dues. This way you do not have to overburden your existing financial liabilities and you are free of all pressures to sell the property. Even if you do not make any profit from such a break-even situation, you now have a property against which to command a superior credit rating for the next venture. You are also in a position to take advantage in your income tax returns by claiming certain expenses as legitimate deductions. I shall come back to this matter a little later in a separate chapter.

The ideal thing to do, then, is to rent out the property. This is the first step to building your assets, capital stock and access to the much needed capital for future ventures.

As I said earlier, try to locate properties that are in need of minor repairs, and buy them cheaper. Once you have such a property, undertake the necessary repair work, thus increasing the property value almost immediately. Then, if you wish, you can put it up for sale—even in a buyer's market, you stand to gain a modest profit. But you will find that these little profit margins are not worth the trouble in the long run.

Before you make such decisions, sit down with a pencil and paper, write down the details of all expenses and assess them against the income. Examine their implications and impact on your overall income and liability situation. If it works out heavily against you, then it may be wiser to sell the property. But situation such as this is very rare, if for no reason other than a faulty planning to begin with.

If this does seem to be the case, you will be well advised to sell the property to minimize and contain your losses, and start once again from the beginning.

The conventional wisdom suggests that a time lag of three to five years should be allowed between the time a property is bought and eventually sold. The intervening period is dedicated to rental income and plough back a portion of such incomes to upgrading the property value. Needless to add, there should be enough flexibility to take advantage and to respond to any favorable changes in the market place. An income-generating property is generally attractive to potential buyers.

Consistent with the decision or plan to build a solid real estate investment portfolio, the objective is to buy more and sell less and to sell judiciously. I have mentioned earlier, be contrary to current trends. Buy when every one is selling and sell when not too many are selling. As you operate in the market under the prevailing market conditions, try to influence it to the best advantage for yourself. With more properties in your possession or in your holding, you can do just that.

However, if you do decide, for personal reasons, to be in the market simply to buy and sell, you can do so, at times, on the same day and even before closing and transferring the property in your name. This is called land flipping. In order to do this kind of deal,you try to close the deal at a maximum possible later date that is convenient to both the parties involved. It is also important that you have the vendor's agreement and cooperation while you bring in prospective buyers to show the property. Behave as though you already own the property, indicate the changes and/or renovations that are being done or will be completed—all these in keeping with the higher prices you expect to command—before or by the time you close the deal with "your buyer". This is a little tricky, as you can well imagine. Here is Mr. X, the original owner from whom you are going to buy the property at an agreed price, and there you are with a client, to whom you wish to sell at a price higher than the price you have agreed to pay Mr. X. How do to you prevent Mr. X from grabbing your client and selling the property to him instead of to you? Draw up the agreement but don't close the deal is one way to protect yourself from such a situation. The other is to make your plans for renovations openly known, thus establishing your expectations for a higher selling price on the property.

Some years ago, some relatives of a friend came to Ottawa from Nairobi, Kenya, seeking investment properties. Initially, they were looking for banking and trust opportunities. I was at that time aware of some problems being encountered by developers and builders of Toronto Lakefront housing development. On my suggestion, the visitors from Nairobi purchased 2500 units at about $25,000 per unit. The builders needed the cash and to unload some of these units. Today, these units are worth in excess of $150,000 each.

Whether you decide to sell a property outright or decide to hold it as a rental property, it is necessary that you undertake some changes and/or renovations to increase its attractiveness as well as market value. If you are going to rent it, explore the possibilities of converting it to a multiple dwelling unit. Such a changeover will not only increase your rental income but the value of the property as well when you eventually put it up for sale. All of these are, of course, subject to your cash flow situation and capacity to withhold and wait. If such capacities are lacking, then you do have to sell. Look out for a good offer that does cover your initial capital investment plus all the costs incurred while doing cosmetic renovations. Your profit may not be high but you will come out even or perhaps a little better than even. And you, my friend, go back to the drawing board and plan for the next venture, based on what you have learnt in the first business. The fact that you have been forced by circumstances to sell rather than wait is symptomatic of a strategy that is like Swiss cheese—full of holes.

At this point, let me tell you one strange fact: you do not necessarily make a profit when you sell a property, you make a profit when you build it—at a price lower than the current or the future market value. The price differential between what you paid and what you are paid is the padding on the profit you have already made.

To increase and thicken this padding, you must, if you can, hold on to your property. Even if the market is sluggish, that is, property values are low, be sure to remember that the real value of the properties are always increasing—you see, land does not grow, it becomes scarce all the time. Only the flurry of activities, whether buying or selling of properties, does so artificially and for a time, reflecting on the going prices. Let this not be a concern of yours, especially when you happen to be the seller. In other words, set your own trend rather than following the market trend. Your own agenda and priority, if set carefully, will come out the winner in the long run.

Be sure and remember, you are there to ensure your future security and comfort without straining your present status.

The only way you can do so is to buy and buy properties as profitably as you can, make them over to increase their market worth, rent them out in a way that cover mortgage and other related expenses, and simply stand back and watch them grow. Some 15 or so years ago, a friend bought 50 acres of a barren farmland for $6000 just out of city limits, in the east end of Ottawa. He bought this property from a needy farmer at, what you may say, fair market value of those days. Today, with all the expansions going on in that area, my friend is constantly offered millions by the developers. Last I heard, he still owns the property and plans to build houses there. Whatever he does, he has a gold mine in his hands. If, on the other hand, some of these properties fail to cover for themselves, you have to reexamine and discover the reasons why, and correct them to become income-generating units. If all these fail, you have to sell them.

While selling them, put yourself in the buyer's shoes. Ascertain what will attract the potential buyer and what will persuade him to accept a given price. Having determined these and similar other factors, add these features and highlight them for visual impact upon all potential buyers. For instance, a patio—either in the backyard or at front—is a good selling point. Or, a finished or semifinished basement work room or recreation room is an attractive added feature. A brighter, less cluttered kitchen area or a tastefully appointed bathroom can be a good selling point.

These improvements or renovations or additions are relatively less expensive but they do increase the attractiveness and, hence, the property value, at a disproportionately higher rate. In addition to this, if you can convert a single occupancy house into a multiple or even a rooming house, the value of the property will increase by two to threefold over the price you have paid. Add to that, if you wait a few years, you can also count on the natural rate of growth in property value in your final profit margin.

All property owners, big and small, concur that time alone is a great booster of property values. The house that I bought in 1972 for some $35 thousand increased in value to over $150 thousand in 1983, without the benefits of any renovations, real or cosmetic.

This is a typical case for all property owners, not a case of my being lucky. It is estimated by various real estate boards that such increases are natural and go up by some 5–10% each year under normal market conditions; these increases may go up to 100%, depending upon extraordinary demand conditions and off-shore investment booms.

To ride on top of these waves—high or low—you must develop an instinct. You can do that by being an avid student of the real estate market. You can become one by being constantly in touch with this market. You can do that by visiting the properties on sale in your area of operation, your target area, and by keeping abreast with housing market in general through newspapers and bulletins issued by the real estate boards and agencies along with government studies and bank reports. All of these are available in your neighborhood public libraries and most of them are available to any one for free or at minimal costs.

Above all, you must cultivate patience and muzzle the temptation for a quick buck. The foundation of a fortune, however small or big, cannot be built on impulse. It demands prudence, patience, deliberate assessment of the market, and capacity to take decisive action when needed or when the time is right.

What I am trying to say is that, all things being given, one is better off holding a property for a few years in which to add a few features that will go a long way in increasing the property's resale value, above and beyond the normal value appreciation of the property. If for some personal or economic reasons, a quick turn-around and resale is a must, then you must add some inexpensive cosmetic changes to attract and justify a price higher than that you paid. These cosmetic changes can and do vary, depending upon a property's present state and status. A simple paint job, tidying up of the back and front lawns, renovation of the basement, the bathroom or the kitchen, fixing up the garage, etc., are some of the less expensive areas where you can expect a higher rate of return for the investment of time, labor and money.

Let us recapitulate now what we have discussed here:

(1) If you do not know already, decide whether to sell or hold the property you have just acquired.

(2) If you decide to sell right away, make specific and firm arrangement with the vendor to facilitate the "viewing" of the property by your prospective clients.

(3) Undertake some visually impressive and attractive renovations and changes to attract a higher sales price.

(4) Try to prolong the closing date while you put the property back in the market.

(5) Should you decide to wait, look for tenants; undertake renovations.

(6) The asking rent should cover, at the minimum, the costs of mortgage payments and other operating expenses, if possible.

(7) Consider conversion of single dwelling into a multiple occupancy unit.

(8) Renovate and increase the future real value.

(9) Have patience.

CHAPTER 10

Management

Now that you have the ownership of one or more real estate properties, and, perhaps, you have rented them out, you have to think about and organize a systematic, efficient management scheme.

Property management is like tending to your garden; you have to lookout for and oversee the upkeep as well as the continued well-being and development on a continuing basis. Nurture and tend to your property and it will return tenfold dividend when you sell. A well-kept, smoothly functioning property, be that single or multiple dwelling, is attractive and tempting to prospective buyers.

Property management also involves — more importantly perhaps — a well-organized management of the accruing incomes (from rent) and expenses (upkeep, administration, etc.). It is also in this area that you begin to recap the harvest of tax-exemption benefits (which is literally money in the pocket) even before the property is sold.

These management areas are not at all complicated. They are simple and are mostly based on organized common sense.

The best way to approach this matter is to identify and separate the two involved management functions distinctly. The first one relates to the properties and their physical environment, and the second one involves the book-keeping system, accounting for all incomes and expenditures—however small—relating to the properties.

It is good to make a note that such procedures should be made separately for each property unit. That way you have at your fingertips the state of health of each of your properties. Such a system also lightens the burden of managing significantly.

Let us take up the management of physical upkeep of the properties first. You will remember, it is very important to make a careful note of the necessary and possible changes that may increase substantially the market value of a prospective real estate property. And they also significantly improve the prospects of easy and quick rental, at a higher rate at that! These changes and/or modifications may be small, or major, or even simply cosmetic. Furthermore, these changes may take place on the physical appearance of the property, such as a paint job, the roof, the patio, etc., or within the property, such as flooring, walls, etc., or may just need grooming and trimming of the yards and mowing the lawns or paving the driveway. Remember, these repair costs are tax-deductible, if the properties are rental units. If you are not sure, check with your accountant.

Once these have been noted and taken care of, you may rent the property. This is done quite simply, by word of mouth or by placing an ad in your local newspaper or by advertising on the bulletin board in your local supermarket and even at your work place.

It is very important to screen a prospective tenant. Check up on his or her employment status and history, past residences, the family unit and composition. These are all perfectly legal queries and a prospective tenant may raise no objections, unless he or she has something to hide.

As for rent, you may recall, that the monthly rent should, ideally, cover your monthly mortgage payments plus prorated property taxes. It is a good idea to let the tenant pay for the utility charges. It is also a good precaution against unnecessary bothers and headaches to make arrangement with the tenant that any minor repairs or replacements should be reported to you (by telephone or in writing) and then to get the job done and the necessary bills sent to you for disbursement either to the tenant to or to the repair person. You may also encourage the tenant to undertake any renovations that are likely to improve the future property value, either through sharing the cost of raw materials or through appropriate adjustments in the rents, for minor repairs carried out by the tenant.

A happy tenant makes a happy property, a happy property enriches the landlord.

It is conventional to take a deposit of the rents for the first and the last month of the lease, as security precautions, to be adjusted over the time of lease.

At this point, it is a good idea to let you know that property rental business is not exactly wilderness. There are rules and laws, mostly at the provincial levels, according to which this business, like all others, is conducted. This is necessary not only to protect your interests as the landlord but also to safeguard the interests and welfare of the tenants.

In every province in Canada and in every state in the United States, there are landlord-tenants acts. These acts basically set out the guidelines for rent control, rent regulations and rent review procedures. In Ontario, for instance, there is a Rent Registry Office (RRO) under the Ministry of Housing, where a landlord must register a rental property. The RRO not only assists a landlord in setting a fair rent for a given property but it also acts as arbitration in any disputed future increases in rents and authorizes tax deductions and cost recovery arising from renovations and upkeep of rental properties.

You can get a copy of the local lanlord-tenant act and other useful information material free of charge (and some at minimal costs) by writing to the Ministry of Housing in Toronto.

I think it is a wise move to get hold of these reading materials; it helps you to understand and to get the best

advantage of the system. Let the government work for you, let
the system serve you!

In every city and big towns in Canada and in the United
States, there are many landlord support organizations. They
are like clubs, where people with similar interests get together
informally and support each other in a variety of ways. It is also
wise to join with the local credit bureau (see the attached for
rent application on p. 97, Appendix A).

If there is such an organization in your town, become
a member. If there is none, how about becoming active in
forming such an organization!

Enough of that. Now, to get back to the main track of our
business: management of any business, and that includes rental
properties as well, is above all a matter of personal style. True,
there are systems and systems, but they are the styles of other
people beyond certain basic "must" elements, such as extensive and accurate record-keeping on each and every move that
goes into keeping a property in the rental market. Your personal style in keeping records may be different, but make sure
that you have the records — for your own information and,
most importantly, for tax purposes and for making government
regulations to work for your best advantage.

As you grow in the real estate business, you will come to see
for yourself the advantages of my own suggestion that you keep
a separate and complete record for each of your properties.

Since a tenant is a vital element in real estate rental operation, let us get back to the tenants again.

As you know, it is illegal to refuse anyone access to a rental
property on grounds of race, colour, sex or religion or physical
disability. You can refuse only on grounds of disagreement on
the rental rate, inability of the tenant to pay rent, or similar
matters.

Nevertheless, it is important not to rent out to someone you
may have difficulty in collecting monthly rents or who may be
potentially destructive to your property through carelessness or

sloppy lifestyle. You carefully screen your potential tenant. Even so, you are taking a big chance. You cannot do much about that but by taking a few off your list of prospective tenants, you can do a lot to confine the odds. For instance, you should think hard before falling for the lure of a tenant resident in Canada as a diplomatic personnel. Such personnel in general, and those from the Third World countries in particular, are not, repeat not, subject to the laws of the land. With such tenants, you have to depend entirely on their civility and goodwill; you cannot take them to the court for nonpayment of rents, or for any damages to the property. Although these tenants are good for fair to high rent money, there are many many instances where such monies have not been paid for a long period of time, where the premises have been left in total shambles, and where the landlord is left holding a very large repair bill.

The other category of tenants one must be very cautious of is "single" or a group of singles wishing to share collectively a rented unit. Here, carelessness and disrespect for the property are the major problems. This is not to say that this is a common practice with this type of tenants, but you can never tell until it is too late. Prevention is safer and better.

The acceptable, problem-free, tenant category is composed of people with family, with job and with credibility, the kind of people with whom you can identify good fellowship and rapport, if you want to.

In any event, this rapport is a very important element in tenant-landlord relationship. A friend of mine bought a new house a few years ago and then, suddenly, he got posted abroad for a duration of two years. He had to rent out his furnished home for that period. When he returned, his house had a superbly finished basement, complete with a wet bar and an extra bedroom, with ensuite bathroom. And all of these was done by the temporary tenant, costing my friend not a penny. Best of all, the tenant offered my friend a choice of attractive options. He offered to buy the house off my friend at a price substantially higher than the original price plus the standard appreciation in value. The other option was also equally generous: the tenant wished to continue leasing the house on a re-negotiated, higher rental cost.

Naturally, my friend accepted his second option, that is, to renew his tenant's lease at a higher price. He simply shopped around and bought himself another home.

Now, this is an exceptional case of good fortune, there is no question about that. But it underscores the importance of a good tenant in advancing the value of a property. With a good tenant at your side, you achieve more than that. You can get rid of so many time-consuming, money-wasting and generally aggravating problems with lawsuits, collection agencies and, above all, with bothersome problems with the government and rules and regulations governing landlord and tenant welfare!

In order to develop a good rapport with your tenant, and at the same time, to continue to improve the quality and, therefore, the market value of your property, it is a good idea to involve the tenant both emotionally and physically. Since the tenant, rather than you, lives on the premises, the tenant knows better the shortcomings and scope for improvements on the property. Ask your tenant, if he or she is happy there, what improvements, renovations, additions, etc., may increase the living comforts, and offer to do the necessary. And then, ask them if they could do the job, with you providing the necessary raw material. You will be surprised, almost 90 times out of 100, the tenant will jump at such an opportunity to show his talent in workmanship. And you can be sure of one other thing, the tenant will do the job or jobs almost 100 times better than a hired handyman, and you can also be sure, besides his own labor and skill he would kick in his own resources to get hold of "little" things for finer finish rather than "bothering" you with the details. After all, he lives there, doesn't he, and he wants his "home" to look good! You just sit back and watch the quantum leap in the value appreciation of your property.

And you become a fanatic about keeping detailed records of all the work, the materials purchased, the receipts for every phase of the operation and a diligent track of the time spent in each phase of work. Because all of these bits of information will help you lower your tax burden. As you know, the house you live in with your family is not subject to any tax deductions; it is the house or the houses or even apartment that you rent out that enable you to take advantage of all sorts of tax deductions. For some of these deduction claims records and receipts may, and eventually will, have to be presented for scrutiny by the tax man. You will do well to get hold of all the information, guidelines available free, or at minimal costs, from the Federal Government Department of Revenue (Taxation) and your Provincial Government Department of Housing. You have been forewarned!

Pending arrival of these documents that, I am sure, you have already requested, let me very briefly tell you what are the broader deductions you may claim as a landlord.

First, you claim the interests on mortgage, the costs of insurance on the property as well as the municipal taxes.

Second, all reasonable repairs, renovation and related labor costs, standard upkeep costs, etc., are deductible.

Third, also deductible are any and all advertising, publicity and promotional costs that are deemed necessary for generating income.

Fourth, if you, as the landlord, are paying for the utilities such as hydro, water sewage and heating they too are deductible.

Finally, since you now have a business, you need a place from where to conduct the same business. Naturally, you have converted a part, perhaps a room, in your home of residence for such purposes. As a result, all operating costs related to your own home can now be taken as a proportion that is dedicated to the conduct of business and, therefore, tax-deductible. If, for instance, you have a 4-bedroom house and if you use one bedroom as your office, you may, without any challenge, now claim 25% of all expenses, including mortgage interests heat, hydro and telephone bills, as your deductible business expense.

There is nothing illegal here. All of these are legal and, above-board, within the guidelines set out for business by the government. So, take advantage of them. But keep very detailed and up to standard records of all expenses.

By the way, did I forget to tell you that now you may even write off 100% of the expenses on your second car, if used for business only. If you have only one car at this time, well, you can deduct a percentage of total mileage travelled for business, including all operating costs—that include, yes, repair bills, gas bills and insurance costs — as legitimate business expense, deductible under current regulations in all Canadian provinces and in all states in the United States.

If you have some doubts, go ahead and contact a lawyer and an accountant for advice. Their fees — your costs in operating your business — are also deductible. Who says it ain't fun!

CHAPTER 11

Tax liabilities are your friends

One thing to remember about real estate is that every one, including politicians, businessmen, government officials as well as the tax men, have a real estate to come home to. It may be rented or owned; therefore, every one is concerned in one way or another about what happens on the home front. One is concerned about the rise and fall in the housing market, changes in rental costs, the residential or property taxes, you name it.

On an interesting aside, sooner or later, almost everyone who can afford must invest in the real estate market as the nest-egg of the last resort. Businessmen and politicians are, in particular, rather partial to this form of investment because it is safe and guaranteed to appreciate in future value while currently offering a modest income in either psychic or real dollar terms.

It is a motherhood and apple pie type of investment that enjoys protection from money-grabbing taxation and other government-sponsored income-generating policies. Instead, there are policies and programs designed by all levels of government to ease the problems and difficulties in real estate ownership. In Canada, there are First Home Buyer's Incentive Programs, Mortgage Insurance Plans, and an array of such policies and programs that are designed not only to assist in home purchase but as well in protecting the investment. The CMHC, the Canada Mortgage and Housing Corporation, is one of the watchdogs at the federal level. The Ministry of

Housing at the provincial levels is involved in promoting and protecting the housing/real estate sector on day to day basis. The U.S. counterparts, that is, federal and state policies, are very similar to those in Canada. But, while in the U.S. a home owner is allowed to deduct mortgage payments from one's personal income taxes, such privileges are not available in Canada at this time, though Canadian tax policies are designed in such a way that one may take substantive advantages from current tax liabilities without breaking the laws, or even reinterpreting them.

One word of caution: Do not evade taxes; pay Caesar his rightful dues!

This means, do not try to interpret tax regulations just to suit your motives. There are more than enough tax advantages embedded on the regulations. All you need to do, as a first step, is to talk with a tax specialist or an accountant. Get him or her to set up a schedule of deductions and exemptions suiting to and appropriate for your personal and business venture. Follow those guidelines while preparing your tax returns. When there are changes or expansions in your business venture, simply visit the tax specialist or accountant for a redesigned schedule. Such tailor-made schedules are perfectly legal and government-approved; best of all, the access to these specialized service is not too expensive.

Let it be clear that the tax advantages coming from deductions and exemptions, etc., are not to be gained from a real estate that is solely for the owner's principal residence. They are only applicable to business and/or rental properties.

I shall explain this as simply and in broadest terms with the following hypothetical example.

Let us assume that you have a rental property. This fact enables you to keep track of the detailed income and expenditure records, including your driving out to inspect or collect rents from the property. These expenses over the income (if the former is higher than the latter) are considered as negative income and, therefore, deductible. You can deduct the pre-scribed depreciation of the capital stock on your rental prop-erty as you can also deduct the interests on mortgages as legitimate expenses. The same goes for all taxes paid on the property.

These deductions, if worked out with the assistance of an accountant, can make a fair to large bundle of deductions from your tax liabilities on annual income.

The additional advantage is that, since you have a legitimate business operation to run, you can, legally, designate space, say a room, in your principal residence as your business office. As I have mentioned earlier in a previous chapter, having an office to run your business entitles you to take a proportion of all expenses as business expenses. That includes telephone to mortgage interests to heat, hydro-electricity as well as miscella-neous business expenses, such as promotion, bank loans, etc.

All of these are to show you that government policies and programs are friendly to property ownership. Sure, there are all kinds of taxes, and, heaven knows, they keep increasing. If you take a moment to think about this burden, you realize fast that these taxes are used to provide, and to continue to improve, services to properties; the increases, in a large measure, reflect the increasing costs of providing these neces-sary services.

In any event, any and all taxes levied on real estate are reflected in the increasing value of the property at all times. One may even go so far as to suggest that taxation is one of the important factors in rising property values.

Your rent does, or should, keep abreast with increases in taxes, rising costs and the rate of inflation. These are the three most important elements in contemplating rent hikes, with the blessings of regulatory agencies.

Finally, it is simpler and, perhaps, even wiser to make the year-end (that is, the calender year) as your business year, along with the personal income taxation time. That way, you do not have to go through the messy job more than once. Also, for most landlords, a simple business accounting "Income and Expenses" form (available at all Revenue Canada offices) is a sufficient and necessary business income/loss reporting system. It is simple, easy, painless (relatively speaking) and can be used to the best advantage of your taxable income portions.

Any capital gains from your income-generating rental properties are, of course, subject to taxation. As to how to treat this to your advantage such as reduction or withholding etc, the situation differs from case to case. It is prudent to work out a treatment scenario with your accountant.

For the average landlord with, say, one to ten holdings, as I mentioned before, the prescribed and standard Income Tax Returns Form plus the Income-And-Expenditure Form are sufficient.

This brings us to the final phase of our discussion on user-friendliness of our tax liabilities. You may be wondering if you need to incorporate your business. Well, for most real estate investors, my suggestion will be a short, NO.

Incorporation offers bureaucratic mess in a finetuned personal affair and there are untold disadvantages in many shapes and forms. As a starter, it is costly to incorporate; the government regulations are a royal headache and must be complied with; the books have to be kept for regular and irregular public auditing; you have to file a corporate return as an annual report each year, a very expensive and time-consuming proposition; your chances of recovering or spreading any losses are minimal because they are going to be, what they are colorfully known as, trapped in the company, thus disallowing you to deduct them against personal incomes.

Once, however, the business has taken-off and grown to Campeau or Reichman proportions, then you may consider incorporation to reap the big advantages fit for corporate giants.

At the very most, should you wish and be advised by your accountant, you may consider some cosmetic moral booster like "sole proprietorship or partnership" on a piece of paper, depending upon the type of your business. In such situations, there is no need for official registration and any of the wide range of legal obligations faced by incorporated concerns.

Whatever may be your choice, be prepared to follow the first and most important rule of any business: Keep separate, detailed record/account of all incomes and expenses for each venture. Learn to keep them separately in well-organized filing system. Keep all bills of sales and/or receipts related to each transaction.

If you do this, I promise you, there won't be any additional bothersome forms to fill out at income tax time beyond the standard ones we all must every year!

It is also a very good idea to open a separate bank account to deal with your business transactions. Do not use your personal or family account for this purpose.

Finally, if you are hooked on to a public image, go right ahead and pick up some name for your business venture. Check with the Provincial Registration office for a title search to make sure no one else before you has taken the name!) and pay a nominal fee of about $25, one time only, and start using the name. For gratis, you may even call yourself the President or the Chairperson! Are you happy now?

CHAPTER 12

On the road to success

My friend, we have come a long way. We have discussed some of the secrets, the know-hows, of getting into and succeeding in real estate business. I cannot, honestly, claim that these and these alone are the last words or even the sure-fire "tricks" in this business. But they have been useful to me, they have given me a measure of satisfaction, success and security through my own dealings in real estate market.

It is true, of course, that I am not a giant in this field. Why, you may not even have heard of me until this meeting! Well, I am not a giant and that is precisely the reason that I thought of talking to you, of sharing with you the experiences of an ordinary person. You may have noticed that the Trumps or the Campeaus of the world, when they share their knowledge or secret, tend to begin at a point that is already too far ahead of us, we dare not try to reach for that point. The success of these giants is of gigantic proportions and worthy of genius.

I wanted to tell you that, in a way, we all can achieve a little more than what we do on a day to day basis in our lifetime. They are not spectacular in any way, but nor are they imposs- ible dreams.

We all can do it: reach for our own stars!

I have taken the liberty to recount for you how I have reached for my own star and have achieved a great sense of accomplishment, just as you will try to pick up the courage to reach out for your own star. You need not necessarily find my ways right or appropriate for you. If I have succeeded in encouraging you, to light up the challenge in your mind, then,

I know, I have achieved the goal I set out in writing this book.

If I have to sum up all these pages into a snappy, catchy formula for approaching and succeeding in real estate investment, it will have to be:

$$\textbf{Patience } (P) + \textbf{Time } (T) = \textbf{Money}(M)$$

$$P + T = M.$$

This is true, very true, tried and tested in the real estate in particular and in all affairs of business in life. **Let me christen it as Mody's Law!**

Follow the tenets of this formula at each step in any venture or business you embark upon, and surprise, surprise, you will have no chance of failure.

The money in your hand is hard-earned, either by yourself or as a result of someone else's hard work. It is clear that to spend or invest the product of such hard labor, even denial of pleasures, without full or at least adequate information and knowledge is nothing less than criminal irresponsibility.

In real estate, especially, irresponsible actions and moves can spell disaster in one's life. This business, because of its relative ease of entrance and durable, profitable nature, is particularly a choice heaven for flim–flam artists and cooks who are not there waiting to get at the sucker's purse. They have schemes to sell the gullible the Brooklyn Bridge, over and over again. And there are more than enough babes in the wood to buy it again and again.

Have you noticed how many business magnates and politicians, trip over and ruin their fortunes and careers? One thing is common in their misfortunes. It is the real estate deals they greedily get involved with. Remember, the recent Orlikon deal that spelled ruin for at least three prominent Canadians.

Just because real estate business looks to be easy and straight forward does not mean that traps are not laid out at every step of the way. Walk wisely, cautiously and with a map of where you are heading. And mind the rules and regulations that govern the business. If in doubt, you don't have to spend money to step back, get some advice to take a second look. Your banker, the money man, is there anxious to serve you, the real estate brokers are there waiting for your business, an accountant or a lawyer is ready to dole out advice in exchange for future business. Use them every step of the way. There is no such thing as full expertise and total command in any business. Around the corner, there stands a fella who may just be a little smarter to take you for a ride. And, believe me, that won't be a joy ride!

You are now ready for the journey up the road to your own success. As I wish you "BONNE CHANCE", I also want to impress upon that knowledge is more important than money that you will need to reach your goal. During our talk, I have stressed on the ways and means of acquiring such knowledge. They are relatively less painful, they are definitely not expensive. Go to your local public library and read all the material on real estate. Attend seminars, workshops and discussion groups organized by the City hall, the real estate brokerage houses, investment specialists—they are all free of charge. Go out and take a drive through your town, get to know the place like the palm of your hand—it is pleasant. Talk to builders on your visits to construction sites—they will be flattered by your attention. Go and meet your local politicians, the bankers, the professionals—you will make friends who will be useful in your future.

In short, be an allrounder, knowledgeable: make this quest not a painful task but a hobby. This is the most crucial investment that I can think of on the road to success.

Do you recall that we talked about commitment, dedication to your dream and your objective? I suggest, you find a very personal way to review and reinforce this steadfastness, so that all the minor, irritating setbacks, obstacles and failures will not weaken your resolve. In real estate business, these obstacles are encountered in greater numbers and in higher frequency as you start in the business. Do not be discouraged; above all, do not panic. There is always a way out and you will eventually find it.

Before closing this chapter, and this book, I would like to recapitulate 10 (ten) most important rules to provide you with guidance on your way to success.They are also equally appropriate in foreseeing and avoiding difficulties or difficult situations. These rules, let us call them Mody's Rules, while given in the context of real estate business, are just as appropriate in any other business venture.

Mody's Rules:
(1) Trust in your judgement or gut feelings. Do not trust your lawyer, accountant, real estate agent, even your partner (if you have one); but do listen to what they say very carefully. Then take action.

(2) Always be receptive to new ideas, people and information. Widen your circle. Be knowledgeable and up to date in your chosen field.

(3) Be exacting file/record keeper. Record in minute details all the aspects of transactions. Keep separate files for each transaction.

(4) Be on time—with everything dealing with payments, appointments, etc. You will be returned the favor—in time—by others.

(5) Be an expert on government rules and regulations governing your chosen business.

(6) It is your business; do as much work as you can. For the rest, get the best help there is.

(7) Keep your investment or business premises as attractive as possible. Dividend on such investments are extremely high.

(8) Be attentive and caring to the views and concerns of those you do business with.

(9) Remember, money does not grow on trees. Be analytical and frugal,never a miser!

(10) Enjoy the venture. You are not on trail!

GOOD LUCK!

Summation A: Stay on top

(1) Each day, check the newspaper listings on real estate.

(2) Check regularly with real estate lawyers, accountants and brokers about property foreclosures, estate settlements, etc.

(3) Meet regularly your bank manager and/or mortgage officer.

(4) Obtain regularly the documents on government policies affecting real estate business; that includes rent controls, property taxation, reporting procedures, income taxation, etc. .

(5) Have some attractive business cards for yourself for personal advertisement.

(6) Attend regularly free-of-charge/obligation seminars and workshops on real estate business.

(7) Take regularly a pleasure-cum-fact-finding drive through the city or town you live in, especially focusing on the new development areas.

(8) Talk to developers, construction crew and to people who share your interest in real estate.

(9) Always be mindful of improving your credit ratings with financial institutions. Borrow small amounts and repay them before dates agreed upon.

(10) Try to buy a property, however small, on a regular basis.

(11) Check regularly and update your books and financial affairs, share a summary of this check to your bank manager. Your ratings will increase.

(12) Always keep separate, detailed records of all transactions for each property holding.

(13) Prepare a personalized rental agreement.

(14) Establish a cordial, fair-business, relationship with all tenants.

(15) Prepare an established tenant-screening procedure.

(16) Check regularly with tenants about renovation, repair and improvement of your properties. Keep photographic "before and after" pictures. Keep the bills, receipts and records of all works undertaken and completed.

(17) Devise efficient and effective property management system in collaboration with your tenants.

(18) Develop a wide-ranging acquaintance/friendship with a few chosen real estate brokers. This will get you a first crack at some choice new listings as well as inside dope on others.

(19) Develop a communications skill to help you with negotiations.

(20) Always be a sympathetic and caring listener to prospective vendors.

(21) Always deal directly with the vendor.

(22) If you wish to really grow in real estate business, you must not hesitate to make offers on every property you are interested in, no matter how small the offers are or how often they are rejected by vendors.

(23) Trust no one,not even yourself, without sufficient and proven facts and information.

(24) Be genuinely interested and helpful to others. Come through as helpful good samaritan to a vendor or to a tenant, and you have made it.

(25) Try to relax and enjoy the challenge you set for yourself. An intense person is often a bore and, generally, boorish to those he expects to do business with.

Summation B:
Some do's and don't's that worked for me

(1) Remember, the job that you hold will never make you a millionaire. It will guarantee bread and butter on the dinner table as you work to your future potential. So, don't quit that job yet.

(2) Study and take some courses on real estate business.

(3) Cultivate friendship with a diverse and wide range of people with different professional backgrounds and interests. You never know what friendly advice you may need in the future.

(4) Develop an understanding for money. Establish a solid credit rating, personal reputation and good standing with money-menu.

(5) You will, eventually, learn to make money with other people's money. Wait and see.

(6) Do not be afraid to take a calculated risk. Gather all necessary information, shift through them, digest them, and the risk will be minimized, if not evaporated.

(7) Learn to respect time as more valuable than money. And time will beget money.

(8) Be creative in all your transactions, from communication to negotiation to business operation.

(9) Be firm with yourself and with those you wish to conduct business. This does not mean, you be rude. No! You try to keep your word at all times under all circumstances.

(10) Do not, to begin with, go for a big dash. You focus your aim in buying smaller, even poorly maintained, real estate properties, if possible, in relatively good and stable residential areas.

(11) Do not hesitate to make a low offer. You can always increase it. And try to deal directly with the vendor.

(12) Be on the lookout on your own. Ask questions, shift through the responses. And you will have the answer you need.

(13) Always buy real estate when others are selling, that is, when it is a buyer's market and vice versa. Also, buy when the mortgage rates are higher and sell when they are lower. You can command favorable prices.

(14) Remember, in real estate, you generally make money—your profit—when you buy and on the price you pay, not when you sell it, at whatever the price.

(15) Do not buy expensive properties, nor should you buy old (over 25 years) properties unless you are a proficient handyman.

(16) Do remember, a NO is not meant to be a discouragement, it is an incentive to be persistent.

(17) Do establish a good, friendly, personal rapport with your tenants. Make them feel at home and they will willingly protect and improve your investments.

(18) Be punctual in your payments schedules to everyone. The favor will be returned.

(19) Be patient with your real estate investments: real estate prices, like everything else, go up in a cycle of approximately 10 years, following the demand and supply cycles reflected in construction activities. The rate of inflation is another inducer of higher real estate prices; similarly, deflation can ruin everything, including real estate market, at least in the short run.

(20) Once you have established yourself in the business, let go of the primary concern with the choice of location for

your investments, and shift your prime focus on profits alone!

(21) As you grow financially, always remember those who helped you: your lenders, your brokers, your tenants, you will be surprised how much help you received from how many people! Be aware of their contributions toward your success. That will save you from unseemly cockiness and keep you modest, if not humble. Protect yourself from downfall that inevitably comes with cockiness.

(22) Always, especially when you are successful, work smarter, not harder. You will have time to enjoy what you are doing.

Summation C. Renting out

PROPERTY ADDRESS: A sample Application for Rent   Date:

		HUSBAND			WIFE		
NAME	FAMILY FIRST		Childern				
AGE		D	M	Y	D	M	Y
S.I. #		—		—	—		—
Address	FROM —— M Y TO —— M Y		Tel:		MONTHLY RENT $		
	FROM —— M Y TO —— M Y		Tel:		MONTHLY RENT $		
	FROM —— M Y TO —— M Y		Tel:		MONTHLY RENT $		
JOB	PRESENT JOB FROM —— M Y		Tel:				
	FROM —— M Y TO —— M Y		Tel:				
	FROM —— M Y TO —— M Y		Tel:				
	Occupation						
LOAN			Tel:				
			Tel:				
CAR	YEAR MAKE COLOUR LICENCE CAR SERIAL # DRIVER LICENCE # PLATE #						
RELATIVE		Tel:					
FRIEND		Tel:					
LANDLORD	FROM TO		Tel:				
Bank		Tel:					
OTHER INFORMATION							

Sample rental agreement form

APPENDIX B

Agreement between _____ , owner(s) and _____ Tenant for dwelling located at _____.

Tenant(s) agree to rent this dwelling on _____ basis for $ _____ per month, payable in advance on _____ day of every calendar month. When rent is paid on or before the _____ day of calendar month, Tenant(s) may take a $ _____ discount from rent.

The first month's rent is $ _____ , due on _____ . The last month's rent or damage deposit is $ _____ , due upon signing this agreement.

Tenant(s) will give _____ day's notice in writing before they move and will be responsible for paying rent through the end of the notice period or until another tenant approved by the owner has moved in, whichever comes first.

Only the following persons (and pets) are to live in the rented dwelling _____

_____

No other person (or pet) allowed.

The use of the following is included in the rent

_____

_____

Tenant pays for the following _____

_____

_____

Tenant agrees to the following:

(1) Keep the yards and garbage areas clean.

(2) Avoid creating disturbances for other tenants and in the neighborhood.

(3) Not to paint, change or alter the dwelling without owners written permission.

(4) Park in designated space.

(5) Allow owner to inspect the dwelling or show it to prospective buyer, appraiser, contractor or other tenants at any reasonable time.

(6) Cheques must be good when paid or no discount will be granted. Any NSF cheques bears a penalty of 2% of face value on cheque.

(7) Pay for all damages caused by Tenant and or his guests.

Violation of any part of this agreement or nonpayment of rent when due shall be cause for eviction under appropriate sections of the applicable code, and the prevailing party shall recover court costs and reasonable legal fees involved.

Tenant hereby acknowledges that he has read this agreement, understands it, agrees to it, and has been given a copy.

Owner: _____   Tenant: _____
Date: _____   (Spouse): _____

Summation D.
Worksheet on buying/selling

APPENDIX C

PURCHASE/SELL AGREEMENT CONDITIONS

Purchaser(s) _____

Vendor(s) _____

Through _____

Premises on _____ side of _____ Municipal No _____

Legal Description _____

City of Ottawa/Township of _____ Frontage _____ Depth _____

Price _____ Deposit_____

CDM unit _____ Level _____ Cond Corp No _____

---

1. The Purchaser agrees to assume the existing First Mortgage held by _____ in the amount of approximately $ _____ , bearing interest at the rate of _____ % per annum, and repayable _____ (Plus 1/12 annual property taxes), and maturing _____

---

2. The Purchaser agrees to assume the existing Second Mortgage in the amount of approximately $ _____ held by _____ bearing interest at a rate of _____ % per annum, and repayable _____ and maturing _____ .

---

3. This Offer to Purchase is conditional upon the Purchaser being approved as a borrower by the mortgage _____ within _____ days of the date of acceptance failing which this offer shall become null

and void and all deposit money shall be returned to the Purchaser without interest and neither the Vendor nor the Agent shall be liable.

4. The Vendor agrees to take back a (First) (Second) Mortgage for $ _____ bearing interest at the rate of _____ %, repayable _____, and maturing _____ (Or on the date of resale at the option of the Mortgagee) (The Purchase: is to have the privilege of paying all or any of the Principal balance without notice or bonus at any time.

5. The Purchaser agrees to pay the balance of the Purchase price, subject to adjustments, in cash or by certified cheque to the Vendor on closing.

6. This Offer to Purchase is conditional upon the Purchaser or the Agent being able to arrange within _____ clear days of the date of acceptance of this offer, Saturday and Sundays excepted, an increase in the existing First Mortgage held by _____ of not less than $ _____ , to bear interest at a rate not more than _____ % calculated semi annually not in advance, amortized over _____ years to run for a term of _____ years and repayable by monthly payments of approximately $ _____ including blended principal and interest, failing which this agreement shall become null and void and all deposit money shall be returned to the Purchaser without interest and neither the Vendor nor the Agent shall be liable.

7. This Offer to Purchase is conditional upon the Purchaser or the Agent being able to arrange within _____ clear days of the date of acceptance of this offer, Saturday and Sundays excepted, a (new) (First) (Second) mortgage for not less than $ _____ to bear interest at a rate not more than _____ % calculated semi-annually not in advance, amortized over _____ years, to run for a term of _____ years and repayable by monthly payments of approximately $ _____ including blended principal and interest, failing which this offer shall become null and void and all deposit money shall be returned to the Purchaser without interest and neither the Vendor nor the Agent shall be liable. This condition is for the benefit of the Purchaser and may be waived by him at his option at any time within the above time limit.

8. This Offer is conditional upon the written approval of the Purchaser by _____ on or before _____ failing which this agreement shall become null and void and all deposit money shall be returned to the Purchaser without interest and neither the Vendor nor the Agent shall be liable. This condition is for the benefit of the Purchaser and may be waived by him at his option at any time within the above time limit.

---

9. This Offer is conditional upon the Purchaser completing a binding agreement of Purchase and Sale on his property at _____ and notification of such agreement being given to the Vendor or the Agent by signed waiver of this condition no later than _____ , failing which this agreement shall become null and void and all deposit money shall be returned to the Purchaser without interest and neither the Vendor nor the Agent shall be held liable. This condition is for the benefit of the Purchaser and may be waived by him at his option at any time within the above time limit. Provided that the Vendor may still offer the property for sale to other prospective Purchasers, and in the event of him obtaining another acceptable offer, he shall notify the Purchaser herein, in writing, delivered in person or by registered mail, or by telegram to the Purchaser at the Purchaser's last known address. Within (_____ days) (_____ hours) from receipt by the Purchaser of the notice aforesaid, the Purchaser herein may waive the contingent clause in said (_____ days) (_____ hours) period and proceed with the completion of the transaction. Unless the Purchaser elects to waive the contingent clause as stated, the Vendor shall be free to accept an offer from another Purchaser and refund the deposit money paid with this agreement and neither the Vendor nor the Agent shall be liable for any damages or cost.

---

10. This Offer to Purchase is accepted by the Vendor provided that a condition in an agreement between the Vendor and another Purchaser is not waived within (_____ days) (_____ hours) of this acceptance, in which event the Vendor will so notify the Purchaser in writing, and this agreement shall become binding as to all its terms and conditions.

---

11. This agreement shall be conditional upon the Vendor, at his own expense, obtaining severance approval in accordance with Section 29 of

the Planning Act and complying with the provisions of the Planning Act and any amendments thereto.

---

12. If the date fixed for closing of this transaction falls upon a day when the appropriate land registry office is not receiving documents for registration, then this transaction shall be closed on the first business day following.

---

13. The Purchaser is to have the privilege of paying off the whole or any portion of the _____ mortgage at any time without notice or bonus.

---

14. The _____ mortgage shall contain a clause permitting the renewal or replacement of _____ mortgage at any time provided any increase in the principal sum by any renewal or replacement shall be paid in reduction of the _____ mortgage.

---

15. The Purchaser acknowledges that the property is part of a condominium which has not been registered as at the date this Offer is made and that he is purchasing only the Vendor's interest which is subject to the terms of an agreement between the Vendor and the builder underwhich one of the requirements is a monthly payment to the builder of $ _____ until the date of registration. In the event that the declaration, description and by-laws have not been registered in the apropriate office of Land Titles as of the date of closing, the Vendor's Solicitor will hold all purchase monies paid to him in trust for the Purchaser as his interest may appear.

---

16. The Vendor agrees to discharge all existing mortgages or encumbrances, other than any which the Purchaser has agreed to assume, on or before the closing date, at his own expense.

---

17. The time allowance for search of title shall commence from the date all conditions have finally been removed and not from the date of acceptance as shown.

---

18. Provided further, the Vendor may continue to offer the real property for sale, and in the event he receives another offer satisfactory to him, he may so notify the Purchaser in writing by delivery to the Purchaser's address. The Purchaser shall have _____ hours from delivery of such notice to waive this condition by notice in writing delivered to the Vendor, failing which this Offer shall become null and void and the Purchaser's deposit returned in full without interest and the Vendor shall be at liberty to accept a new offer.

19. The Vendor agrees to supply to the Purchaser an up-to-date survey of the said lands, at his own expense, on or before closing.

20. Acceptance of this offer is subject to the (Vendor's) (Purchaser's) solicitor reading and approving this offer within (_____ days) from the data of acceptance of this offer, failing which this offer shall become null and void and the Purchasers deposit shall be returned to him in full without interest or penalty and neither the Vendor nor the Agent shall be liable.

Unless otherwise provided, the real property shall include all appurtenances and fixtures relating to the real property and without limiting the generality of the foregoing shall include storm and screen sash and doors, electric light fixtures, curtain rods and tracks, all such as are presently on the real property excepting the following items which are not included in the Purchase price (hot water tank is rented)

allowed for title search _____ days. Closing & Possession date: _____ offer irrevocable until _____ am/pm _____

CDM. What is the condominium fee per month $ _____ and it includes: